Also by Terry Elston

THE ABC OF ABUNDANT LIVING

INSPIRATIONAL & MOTIVATIONAL QUOTES

THE TEACHERS GUIDE TO NLP

KNOWING NLP

-The Real Understanding Of It -

TERRY ELSTON

NLP World
First published in Great Britain 2010
By Terry Elston
www.nlpworld.co.uk

KNOWING
NLP

Dedicated To:
Jo Wright for her diligence, Ben
Bonetti for his passion for success
and assistance, Craig Fourie for his
quality work. All practitioners of
transformational work, including
John Overdurf for his persistent
commitment to opening doors on
perceptions to change.

Index

Introduction

I wrote this book to assist a greater understanding of the art and science called Neuro Linguistic Programming (NLP); and from this understanding, fill a gap that I perceive exists from people wanting to know more about the knowledge and wisdom inside NLP.

This book is also for those who have been trained in NLP to gain a deeper understanding of what they think they know is NLP!

The intention is that by the time you finish this, or even before, you'll have a greater perception and perspective of the principles and techniques on parade.

One of the most difficult questions to answer is the basic learner's initial comment "what is NLP"? Yet even experienced practitioners should still be asking that question! To answer it, we will have to uncover what underpins the thinking and being of a skilled practitioner.

Some of the secrets I'll broach in this book will surprise you and shock you. The purpose is to show you what's behind all of the principles that have been trained over the last 35 years since its inception.

Many NLP trainers may also be surprised to find that what they teach isn't actually NLP at all. Just what was marketed as NLP! The very basis of the techniques came before the skill sets themselves; just by default, before the techniques were here, there were none! During this journey into the heart of NLP, we'll explore what makes NLP work, what's behind it and how you can apply it.

As well as this being an informative book, I will give you plenty of chances to use the concepts here, so you can experience the process of NLP at the same time as reading about it.

To begin, let's uncover the very title itself.

NEURO. This refers to all the neurons in the body and the ability of the mind and body to communicate with each other. There are so many possible neurological connections available in the mind and body that it would be impossible to count them. Some have said as many as the number of stars that are in the sky.

Anything happening in the mind also happens in the body and vice versa. Again, from studies by Deepak Chopra (1989), he cites the neurotransmitter as being the communication device of the mind. These neurotransmitters are bathing every cell in your body. Therefore every cell is listening intently to every thought emitted from your mind!

This has particular implications on your body language. There is a saying in NLP that you cannot - not communicate. That's because your deeper mind will always be commenting on something and showing it through the body. Really, the body can't lie! We all give off unconscious signals that other people pick up on.

How this is useful is to start to become aware of your own signals through your body (remember that another person will be more inclined to believe your body language than your words). You can then also start to be more aware of another's unconscious signals, and start to master the knowledge of the 'unseen' world of communication.

Which brings us onto the word LINGUISTIC, which is then all the verbal and non-verbal translations of the inner world. The transmission of all that data has to come out of your mouth or your body. Either you are doing the communicating overtly or covertly!

Lastly, the word PROGRAMING describes the patterns that are inside us all (also called *filters* in NLP). The basic premises being that we are all programmed at an early age and have to deal with those patterns, until we can be free of them and regain some independence.

Here are some of the interpretations you may have heard when listening to the description of the art and science of NLP:

* magic of the mind
* a set of processes that consistently cause change
* a toolbox of transformational techniques.

Knowing these descriptions of NLP, what is it really?

NLP is reported as being an ART as well as a SCIENCE for good reason: Firstly, you can consistently expect the same (or very similar) results when approaching problems or challenges.

Personally, I can predict that 9 out of ten phobias I treat, will be gone within 30 minutes. That could be with complete strangers with no previous experience of NLP. You cannot fake or pretend a 'proper' phobia gone, so when tested, it's either there or not! That's the scientific side to NLP. It's measurable and consistent. The one out of ten would also have the phobia removed; it may just take a little longer for that one!

The ART side to NLP is in the approach. Even though the structure to NLP can be classified as scientific, the way different Practitioners tackle an issue can be universes apart! I deliberately put my previous experiences of success away when meeting a new client, as I cannot possibly predict what method will work with another human being.

I have had situations where the client has literally healed themselves just by turning up to my studio! What replicable scientific method was present on those occasions? Which brings us to the answer of what is happening in the dynamic of practitioner and client in any learning, therapy situation.

If you think of the client as a seed of possibilities, or even just as a seed; your environment (i.e. your studio, your training room), will act as a womb (from which the word room has come in the first place) and therefore the clients will begin to heal themselves or at least assist greatly in the transformational process.

This we cannot measure and is not scientifically provable. I can just assert that when my preparation of my own mind, my clients' mind and the training room or studio has been immaculately prepared, the transformation of people is a whole lot easier!

Prelude
Prepare for change!

The preparing of a room is something I learned a long time ago whilst working for a self-development company. I saw the results they were getting from their introductory evenings outstripped anything else I'd seen in relation to signing up for paid courses.

I realised that the trouble they took preparing the environment caused a concentration of mind and a presupposition that the arena was different.

To start with, you have to completely clear the room of anything that isn't to do with the training or situation at hand!

Take out any newspapers, books, cups, ornaments (that don't have to do with the context at hand), tables chairs that are superfluous and even pictures that don't play any role in what's happening in that session. All of these things will be 'clocked' by the unconscious mind and detract from the power of the meeting.

Before the session, you will have given your client (or the people on the training) a series of ordeals to perform that lets them know something big is about to happen. In accordance with the metaphor earlier, the seed is being prepared!

With your room/studio or training room set up perfectly with no distractions, you are already on a winning wicket.

The other preparation can be done before they get there.

With my NLP trainings, the delegates have mp3s to listen to and a test to fill out. It's always funny to watch peoples personalities deal with the ordeals. We all attempt to do the ordeals in our own way: If we have a rebellious past, we won't do the test at all or if we don't complete things, we won't complete the test!

All these feedbacks are great markers for you to be able to interact with that personality before the session or training to weed out that behaviour before you see them. You simply point out the deeds they are displaying and ask them about their patterns in life. Most people are quite happy that you interact on this level and that their behaviours are 'busted' at this time.

From your side, make sure you have cleaned out your own cupboards in life before seeing the person or people. Do your 'washing up' in life and make sure you are as 'complete' as possible with your life situations. Do your preparation for the session in good time and look to see how you can improve from the last time. Then it's time to focus and vision the sitting into existence. Perhaps meditate on the session in hand; you can pick up an immeasurable amount of information when you tune in, in advance of your meeting.

Chapter 1
The Human Communication Model: The Edges of Reality

I think what NLP has done for most of my clients over the years, is to give them a different perspective of life and reality. It has beautifully defined the equipment we use to judge ourselves and the outside world, plus given us new ways of viewing life when old ways are not working.

To be able to see things newly, old concepts and patterns have to be transcended. Yet if life is real, how can we do that without just pasting whitewash on black tiles?

The world of our senses can only handle about 7 bits of information per second, give or take about 2 pieces (7 + - 2 from the research of Mihaly Csikszentmihalyi and the book The Magic Number 7, George Miller).

Therefore what we call reality has been chopped up because we can't handle the amount of sensory data coming in.

Human beings are bombarded with sensory stimuli all of the time. We cannot possibly respond fully to every stimulus we receive, so to cope we filter out a lot of the information coming to us by deleting, distorting and generalising the data (life).

When we receive information (and you will be doing this right now), we try to compartmentalise it into a format we are comfortable with. Our brain will be looking for models that it is already familiar with that it can parallel the information it is receiving.

Once we have sent the information through the filter sieve in our brain, and have checked it against our existing values, beliefs, attitudes, memories and language systems, we construct an internal representation of the information received. Simultaneously a state is created which will be evident from our physiology, and we exhibit certain behaviours.

Knowledge of how a person filters data can help you understand them and also, if taught appropriately, allows the person to understand themselves. We filter life by generalising, deleting and distorting it.

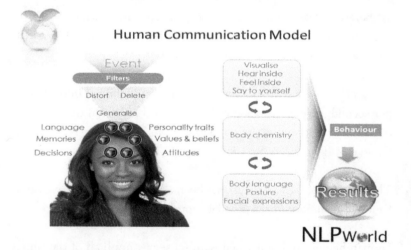

Generalizations

From infancy, we are trying to cope with the world around us. To do this we make a lot of generalizations. This is a useful strategy as once you've learned how a door works, it's good to generalise this to other doors so we don't have to learn newly every time we are faced with the challenge of opening one!

Deletion

You don't have to go far to know this is true; our Swedish trainer, Susanne Billander deleted a whole train as she sat waiting for it after it stopped in front of her! How many of you have deleted the glasses that were sitting on top of your head whilst looking avidly for them?

Because we receive so much information, we also employ a deletion strategy that helps us to filter out a lot of information because otherwise we'd all go crazy! There's more information coming into your senses as you read this than you can possibly imagine. The research by Mihaly Csikszentmihalyi (1991), tells us that over 2,000,000 bits of information are coming in to your systems every second!

To make this stand out, on the gross level of the senses, as I sit here writing this, I can hear some quiet noises around me. As I make myself aware of them, I realize I am listening to a computer fan, the fridge humming in the next room. Yet before that new awareness, I heard nothing consciously.

To take that assumption further: All around me, there are micro wave, infra red, high frequencies plus all the tiny pixels in every centimetre of space that I am not aware of! However, I have been deleting these noises/pictures/feelings before my conscious mind even became aware of them. It means I can carry on with my focus on this work and not be distracted by extraneous information.

Of course some people and especially some clients, particularly those with ADHD, may find this very hard to do and will keep getting distracted by all this information. Other people actually need 'stuff' in the background to help them concentrate.

Distortion
Look at the following diagram. Now perhaps you see how easy it is to generalise the situation before really appraising it.

NLPw●rld

What this is really telling us is that the world that we experience is not the world that is outside of us; it is a world that we are creating inside. We do not experience reality as it is, we only experience our own perception of reality. Since we all have more or less different sets of filters (that being different sets of values, beliefs, memories etc.), we will all have our own unique perception of the world.

This therefore explains how one person can perceive an event completely differently than another person who has experienced the same event.

What is interesting about this from an NLP point of view is that if our internal representations (our perceptions) of reality are based on our filters, then what we could do in order to change our experiences of the world is simply to change our filters. We are actually in charge of how we perceive reality.

At this point, your question might be "How on earth do I change my filters?"

The whole idea of NLP is based on the fact that everything we do in life has a processes to it, and if we know how we do these processes, we would also know how not to do them and how to replace them with procedures that serve us in a more positive way.

Now we understand that reality is literally made up via deleting, distorting and generalising, the only question left is: What reality would you like in your life?

Chapter 2
The Presuppositions of NLP

Here's where the presuppositions of NLP came into existence. As no reality is totally 'true', we can have any one we like from the jamboree bag of choices available.

NLP has come up trumps with a series of empowering belief systems (or convenient beliefs) that empower us before we even interact with our clients or open our mouths to speak.

Even though no belief is true (positive or negative), having convenient assumptions in the background can totally empower a practitioner. They certainly are more useful than the rubbish that's normally lying around an unkempt mind, that's for sure!

I had a few unkempt habitual presuppositions, which used to trip me up time after time. Here are a couple of them: 'Life's not fair', 'everything will turn out going badly' etc. Don't get me wrong; I wasn't a depressive soul, yet under pressure, this family of linguistic managing agents would parade themselves.

Let's have a look at the presuppositions of NLP. If you study them carefully and really get them into your system, they come alive and are incredibly empowering and enlightening.

To put this into context, these are not positive thinking patterns;

they are powerful philosophical places in which to reside.

NLP Presupposition 1 - The map is not the territory - The menu is not the meal

Our senses take in raw data from our environment and that raw data has absolutely no meaning whatsoever other than the meaning we choose to give it. This is an idea derived from Alfred Korzybski who developed general semantics theory.

We don't actually eat the menu, it is simply a representation of the meal and very useful as a guide to what were are about to eat, but it is not the real thing: It differs in many ways – it's on paper or a board for a start, it is flat and not generally edible. Of course this is just a metaphor, and the real meaning is that each one of us has our own interpretation of the reality 'out there' i.e. the environment we find ourselves in; we understand reality according to our map or menu. We need this 'map' and could not function without it, but we also need to remember that maps and menus need to change over time; they need to be redrafted when we discover a new bit of 'reality' or our palate changes and we need a new menu.

Your mind is also a map. What you make up in there is not actually true; just a representation of reality.

NLP Presupposition 2 - There is no such thing as failure, only feedback

I used to think that life was unfair and unjust. All life was filtered through this veil and even if things were going well, I used to perceive that sooner or later the trap door was going to open to failure yet again.

When I took my NLP training, I realized I had been living out of that negative presumption about life. We did an exercise in the training room and after that, life was different! I had an oversight of my life and then saw that life is not about having to 'win' always; life is about a process of experiences and experiments, all leading to more learning and more experiences.

When life is seen as a learning experience and not just about getting things 'right', the people around you can relax more into the feeling of getting feedback to encourage more excellence in what they do.

I exhibited this on an NLP training. I asked someone to come up who thought they were terrible at catching balls. She proved it by dropping simple catches. I then asked her to stop 'trying' to catch the ball and focus instead on which way the ball was spinning as it approached her. I threw the ball twice as hard and slightly above her head. She caught it in one hand!

When the emphasis is just on 'winning' or getting it right, people tend to drop more balls! What we need to focus on is the process in hand and the feedback about what's missing if it isn't going the way we want it to go.

The deeper mind (which will be in charge of the catching) does not like being challenged too strongly or negatively. If you praise something about behaviour first, then layer in what can be improved, (not what was wrong), you'll keep the baby, the bath water and the bath itself!

Some of this will be challenging to you as a teaching/training provider to change some of your own internal language. Changing habits is like changing your wardrobe. It sounds like a good idea, but sometimes takes a while to get into action. Give yourself (or others) a valuable compliment before layering in some possible changes.

NLP Presupposition 3 - Resistance is a sign of lack of rapport

We will move heaven and earth for those we love and want to impress. When you have rapport you have massive influence. Sometimes in our work we need to act as if we are really connected to the people we work with, even when we feel we aren't.

If you want to get the best out of people you have to really value and cherish them. If you take time to get into rapport, to get into the way they are thinking, you will find communicating and leading them through learning or changing so much easier.

If they resist you, go back and look at your rapport skills (which we will cover technically later on). Think about what you need to do to put them at their ease, to level with them. Make them feel you accept them for what and who they are, that you are meeting them where they are, not where you want them to be. Abraham Lincoln once said, "To defeat an enemy, first make them your friend".

NLP Presupposition 4 - The meaning of the communication is the response that you get

It does not matter what you thought you meant, what matters is what actually results from your words, tone and actions inside other peoples' internal worlds. People respond to their own filter systems, which may be an accurate or inaccurate interpretation of your meaning. To be able to communicate what you mean, you need to have an idea of how the other person communicates. To do that you will have to have tuned into them sufficiently and watched their response.

How frequently have you found what you said has been completely misinterpreted? Stand back, look, listen, feel, get a sense for the other and start to be in their skin, then you can start to get inside what they are understanding or misunderstanding about you and what you said.

It does not matter what you meant, what matters is what the other party feels from what you said. How many times have you said to someone 'I didn't mean it like that!'

You can only change your side of the 2 way communication street, so if your message is not getting across and having the effect you think it should have, you will be flexible enough to change the way you are communicating.

NLP Presupposition 5 - People have all the resources they need to succeed

All the resources we need are inherent in our own physiology and neurology. Even if you can't totally believe that in this moment, it's such an empowering idea to hold on to.

Think about this: When you accept that someone is weak or not powerful in any way, you place yourself in a philosophically corrupt position. Just by rendering them incapable, you put a seal of failure on that person. From now on you have to tend for them, nanny them, condescend to them!

I once got a telephone call from a prospective trainee who wanted to do my 7 day NLP Practitioner course. She asked me if I could help because she was unemployed and had no money. Although it was tempting to drop my price or give her something for nothing,

I resisted and asked her to raise her standards instead. I told her to find some way of making the money, to somehow find something in her system that was powerful and creative.

What happened was three days later she called me to tell me she had the money! She didn't even have to pay it back - it was a gift from a bursary.

What's the message here? Give people the notion that they are powerful, can create from nothing and are resourceful.....and they can be: Give people the notion that they are weak and helpless.... and they will be!

NLP Presupposition 6 - Every behaviour is appropriate in some context

Consider this: No behaviour is wrong in itself; it is perhaps just not the most appropriate way to solve a problem. You can think of it this way: As we go about our business as human beings we are trying to make sense of the world and do the best we can. Essentially everyone wants to be happy; we all seek pleasure. Sometimes though this struggle, the way we get that pleasure will be contrary to someone else's.

Nonetheless, to the doer, it makes some kind of sense. It is worth appreciating this when working with challenging behaviour. Some behaviours really seem destructive and contrary to what a person says that really want. If you, as the therapist or trainer, can suspend your initial reaction and look for a greater intention (see chunking up section), you'll be empowered where you weren't before!

We are not saying we condone the behaviour; we are simply rising above the situation where we ourselves are reacting and not responding.

As an example: Two children are fighting in the playground. The initial reaction is that it's wrong. What if you were to stand back (not for too long of course), and look at what intentions may be behind the behaviours. If one of those kids was fighting because respect had been lost and all they wanted was the respect back (and the friend back), you can easily see that the intention is good (albeit the behaviour destructive).If the teacher in charge was able to view the situation from that place, a resolution could have been paving the way back to friendship, rather than a detention and waiting 30 years to have contact again!

Below are the most popular of the presuppositions of NLP plus a short summary.

The Popular Presuppositions of NLP

• Respect for the other person's model of the world. In order to communicate properly it is important that you have an understanding for the other person's model of the world. All people have different ways of experiencing the world (different beliefs, values, filters, etc.) By understanding and respecting these differences instead of judging, better communication will occur.

• Behaviour and change are to be evaluated in terms of context, and ecology.

• Resistance in a client is a sign of a lack of rapport. (There are no resistant clients, only inflexible communicators. Effective communicators accept and utilize all communication presented to them.) In NLP, being in rapport with the client is crucial! If you are not in rapport, you will not get the positive outcome that you are working towards. In order to get a different outcome you must alter your communication (If what you're doing isn't working, do something different).

• People are not their behaviours. (Accept the person, change the behaviour.) The behaviour a person is acting out is not the person itself, but the person's response to something in their world. What NLP seeks to do, is to enable the person to have more choice in terms of their behaviour and their responses.

• Everyone is doing the best they can with the resources they have available. Behaviour is geared for adaptation, and present behaviour is the best choice available. Every behaviour is motivated by a positive intent.

• Calibrate on Behaviour: The most important information about a person is that person's behaviour. People's behaviour is the only thing we as communicators can observe. Anything else is mind reading. We cannot enter the other person's mind, and it is therefore important to calibrate on behaviour.

• The map is not the territory. (The words we use are NOT the event or the item they represent.) People respond to their experiences, not to reality itself. We do not have access to reality as it is, we do not know reality. We experience reality through our senses, our beliefs, our filter systems, and our own personal "map" of reality. NLP works with changing the "maps" that are not working for the client.

• You are in charge of your mind, and therefore your results (and I am also in charge of my mind and therefore my results). Every action you take has first been a thought in your mind. For there to be an action, there must first be a thought. Nobody but yourself is in charge of your own thoughts, therefore nobody but yourself is in charge of your own results. You are the only person who can change your own results.

• People have all the resources they need to succeed and to achieve their desired outcomes. (There are no unresourceful people, only unresourceful states.) All people have the ability to create whatever they want in their lives. If another person can do it, so can you.
• All procedures should increase wholeness.

• There is ONLY feedback! (There is no failure, only feedback.) There is no need to label our results as failures. Rather, seeing our results as feedback and information that can enable us to seek improvement is far more powerful.

• The meaning of communication is the response you get. The intention you have for the communication is just as important as the response that you get. The response that you get may be different to the response that you wanted. The response is feedback that you can use in order to alter your communication to get the appropriate response.

• The Law of Requisite Variety: (The system/person with the most flexibility of behaviour will control the system.) The more flexible you are, the more opportunities you can take on in your life. If you have boundaries, you restrict yourself. Being open and flexible simply creates more choices in life.

• All procedures should be designed to increase choice. The more choices you have, the freer you are and the more influence you have.

Chapter Three
Sensory Awareness

What we're going to look at now is one of the cornerstones of NLP; one of the cornerstones of any kind of relating, communicating and listening that you'll ever come across.

In NLP we call that Sensory Acuity, or you could call it Sensory Awareness.

Sensory Awareness is so fundamentally important and imperative for any kind of relationship work that you're going to be doing. It's one of the most important pieces of training you'll ever undertake, whether you're a teacher in the classroom, in training rooms, meetings, business, socially, with clients one to one or in your personal relationships.

The bonus points here are given for understanding the language of another's body and be sensitive to that as you communicate. Your client will tell you everything that's going on inside them through their body.

So we are not just talking about how they're sitting, whether their arms are folded or unfolded, or you know whether their head is cocked to one side or another, but everything. I'm talking about the eyes, the breathing, the lips, the colour of the cheeks, whether the breathing is coming from the top or the middle or the lower of their chest. All these are absolute give-aways as to what a person is doing inside.

The way we do this in NLP is not the way that we've seen other factions considering what body language means. This is not a section about what body language means, because body language can mean anything. It's very, very individual.

Of course there can be some generalizations that we can come to in terms of body language, yet we never presuppose a type of body language; breathing, noticing the skin colour can mean anything until we have discovered what that particular behaviour from the body means to that particular person.

That's why this section is a lot different from any kind of body language lesson that you'll ever experience. For instance, if somebody is crossing their arms, it doesn't mean they are closed, or negative or anything at all. They may just be cold....or resting their arms!

But we become so ridiculously habituated into trying to fantasize about what a person's body language means. From everything we've ever heard about body language from the 'experts', we forget to actually look out and see what's happening with that person individually.

What we want to see is if we can notice what that particular body language means in this moment for this person.
Let's say you're with somebody and they get really emotional and sentimental about a certain thing that happened in their life. Now as they do that, their breathing rate will change, the inflections of their voice, their skin colour, how they're moving their hand gestures,

and even their blinking patterns may change as they're talking.

What you're doing at this time, is you're 'clocking' all of this. If any of you have seen the series called Sherlock Holmes, (the contemporary one which started in 2010), it's exactly what we're talking about. He's observing everything.

And with this observation you can make deductions; but only based on how you've seen that person react before. Because what we're saying is people are habitual, so their body language, skin tonus and their breathing is linked to their particular memories and will be consistent for them. And that goes for all of the emotions that this person experiences too.

So first, observe: Observe what comes with that memory, what comes with that particular event they're talking about? Then you are able to decide which particular body language means what to them (and now you of course) now.

What are some of the things that you can start to pay attention to?

We've all got skin colour. The skin colour can be light or dark. Of course in a white person it probably is going to go redder or whiter, in a black person it's going to go darker or lighter, so we can say darker or lighter as a general term.

The skin tonus, which is the tone of the muscles, basically, you'll be able to see some symmetrical, or asymmetrical movement, some tightness or looseness of the muscles.
Breathing. Yes, that's a good idea if your client is breathing. But where are they breathing from, and at what rate?
Of course it does take a fair amount of awareness to be able to

notice where somebody's breathing from, but you can do it. If you're with a female client it's obviously not a good idea to be staring directly at their chest region, otherwise you may lose rapport fairly quickly! Yet you can use your periphery for looking at people too (see chapter on Peripheral Vision or The Hakalau).

When we get into the section on the Hakalau, (also called peripheral vision and the learning state), we'll show you how to do that. But for now just recognise that you can look at somebody's chest without directly looking at their chest. So they'll be breathing either from the top, or the middle, or the lower. Now obviously if the breathing rate is faster it's from the top, medium in the middle, and slower as it gets to the bottom.

You can also look at the lower lip size. You may think that all lower lips are the same size all the time, but no! Sometimes they get bigger and fatter, and there'll be less lines, and conversely sometimes they'll get thinner and there'll be more lines and more wrinkles.

On the image below this same person's lips are fuller on one image and thinner on another

 Lip-Size & Fill

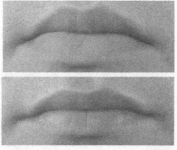

NLPW●rld

You can look at the eyes. The black pupils can be dilated, which is larger, or not, which is smaller. Again, you have to be very aware to pick up on these things, but this is what an NLP practitioner is all about. Awareness.

Be aware of hand movements, these can tell you a whole story! And be attuned to inflections of the voice as well. You can start picking up certain inflections in the voice when they're in certain states, so that you can observe and recreate that in your mind. Make an internal library of what those inflections mean as their voice changes off the norm.

You will be getting a handle on their feelings too. On our NLP Practitioner course, we'll show you how to tune into the feelings. We'll show you how you can pick up on someone's feelings, even with your back turned to them!

On this image the same person's pupils are slightly more dilated in the second image. Yes you have to be *that* aware to pick it up!

 Eye Dilation & Focus

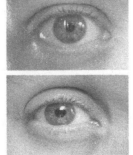

NLPw●rld

Chapter 4
Rapport

How to build excellent rapport

A fantastic place to start on building a good relationship quickly is to attain good rapport with the other person. Basic NLP training provides a toolbox of techniques, which offers ways of doing this effortlessly and unconsciously.

Imagine being able to understand unconscious communication, and how to communicate with the unconscious by using language patterns that make your powers of persuasion hard to resist. Listening to the language people use gives you clues as to how your clients are processing language. If you can mirror their style more accurately, you can enhance your communication with them. You can harmonise with them and draw out the learning more effectively.

The myth of Matching and Mirroring

What most NLP practitioners have been trained in, is something called matching and mirroring. I am going to show you how this works in the next few paragraphs. Before that though, I am going to denominalise it and throw out the myth that it is normally trained as.

What actually happens is that two or more people share energy fields. You can feel if someone else is 'with' you or not 'with' you in energy. You get good 'vibes' (energy vibrations, of course), or not!

That's how you can easily turn your back on someone and still stay very connected (and they will still feel the connection). So the next pieces on matching and mirroring are a little redundant, unless you don't know how to connect with people energetically.

That's not to say that matching and mirroring doesn't work, far from it: In the process of matching and mirroring, at the very least you have to be on the outside, observing them. Then you can't be completely in your own head, without any frame of reference to their body language and state!

So what I am saying is that the natural process of rapport comes from an inner hunger and thirst to really connect.

What is really happening is you are connecting with people energetically. When you recognise that it's the energy that's connecting, you won't have to use your body movements so much to make this happen. The process involved requires intention on your part. To develop energy connections involves wanting to and then making it happen.

I rarely have to 'turn on' my physical rapport techniques because there are normally so many naturally occurring good feelings present in any situation to begin with.

If you can't do that (or that's still not working), then use the processes below.

Mirroring

Mirroring is physically placing your body in the same mirror image of another opposite you (as if in a mirror). This needs to be done with respect and subtlety or will look false and silly. Do not be afraid to use it however, it really does work.

As an example of using the physical version (mirroring), one time my car got towed away from outside my house. It was parked near to a small sign saying, "don't park outside number 23 on Saturday"; but was so small and a similar colour to other signs in the street that I missed it. I decided to dispute it, even though I knew the chances of me winning were very small indeed.

When I got to court, I knew I needed to gain rapport quickly, so I dropped my pen on the floor to see which way the barristers' legs were crossed. I mirrored him exactly. Even though I could only see above the table, the unconscious mind is so smart, it knows if bodies are aligned or not! After a short chat, the barrister was looking with me for extenuating circumstances, so he could get me off the charge!

Of course, there are other aspects of human communication to mirror. On the phone, for example, you don't have any body movements that you can see. What you have is the quality of the voice. You have many aspects of voice to mirror; such as timbre, tone, pitch chunk size of information and volume.

If you have to use physical mirroring, here are some examples of what there is to match and mirror.

- breathing
- tilt of the body
- blinking
- hand Gestures.

Another example of making rapport work positively when I was at Heathrow Airport and needed to only check in hand luggage as someone was waiting in Stockholm to pick me up. The airport assistant weighed my bag and informed me it was 4kg too heavy! I looked at her and smiled, placing my attention on connecting with her and matching her energy and to a certain extent, her body language as well. I said, "What can we do"? She said, "Well it's too heavy". I said, "I know, what can we do"?

She then told me I could put some clothes in my computer bag, but my carry-on bag was still 2kg too heavy. Once more I said, "What can we do"? She looked around and then just waived me on! As soon as I was around the corner I could just put my clothes back in the bag anyhow. Good for rapport!

Leading
The point of matching and mirroring is to eventually lead the situation, whatever that is. When you feel like the two (or more of you) have 'clicked' you can move into the leading phase, because there is enough trust and relatedness. You can't lead any situation if you don't have enough respect/rapport happening with them. They just won't go with you. So just don't even think of leading until the magic of rapport is weaving its way.

What NOT to match

If a person has a bad behaviour or language you don't want to match, then match the energy of the person while using non-confrontational words. A lot of trainers or therapists either try to get louder or quieter than the negatively reacting student. That's a 'mismatch' and will not serve much purpose.

Some people may comment about rapport, "oh isn't that

manipulating? Isn't that false, what you're doing?" Consider this: If you're going to go and meet that friend's baby for the first time, you don't say, "Hello, my name's Terry Elston, I'm a trainer of NLP. Good to meet you. Are you having a good time in there? You look like an awfully nice baby. Bye!"No! You use baby language. "You goo do boo lovely little goo boo joo boo."

That's what you do naturally isn't it? You go into their world, and talk their language so you can be in rapport with them. It's a natural thing to do. It's not, in my world, about manipulation. It's about respect for somebody else's model of the world. You go over there with them.

In saying this, some babies you might not want to match. If you come across some you don't like, you may not want to go and match and mirror them, you might want to avoid them.

Matching
A friend in conversation with another the other day somehow got to talk about walking in step: She said "Have you ever noticed how when we are walking along the street we always seem to be in step with each other, even though we have different sized legs?"

In fact that walk is actually a metaphor for the relationship; this same principle can be applied to other situations, not just walking along the street with a good friend.

When matching, the same leg will be moving in the same time. As you could notice, that feels like fun and you still have the sense of your own identity in that walk, although you'll feel a great deal of camaraderie with the person with you.

When you feel comfortable doing these actions and start to use this technique to gain rapport, you'll realise what a jewel it is! People will feel acknowledged and will appreciate your involvement with them.

Here are some important points

When using energy with clients, closely monitor how much rapport you have and whether your client is losing their own frame of reference and just taking yours.

If using the physical technique, remember: Mirroring builds rapport fast. When mirroring, you can stop mirroring after a few minutes because mirroring is very powerful. You'll probably be leading by then anyway.

Watch out for the lack of referential index (losing themselves), because otherwise they'll stop thinking for themselves and they'll just buy anything you are selling.

The problem is that if they didn't want it really, they'll come back to you the next day being really pissed off. "I didn't want this bloody phone. I wanted..."

Bear in mind that whatever you do comes back. This is part of another conversation, but whatever you put out there comes back. So if you want to rip somebody off, you're going to get ripped off. It's just the way it works. That's the way cycles work.

Matching is easier to pace and you can do it for a longer duration with no side effects. And you only need these techniques if there isn't a natural rapport. Always assume rapport and work the technical side if there is none available naturally.

Group Rapport

A young teacher in her second year of teaching one September described observations of her new class: "They are so different from my last class, I know that they are a year younger, but it has really brought into sharp focus the relationship I had with my old class. I think I can speed up that rapport building by gauging the natural pace of the group, it's almost like finding a kind of 'resonant frequency' for the group, and when I have hit on that I can harmonise with them and the result will be doubly good if I can resonate too."

When we work with groups of people our task is not just to get into rapport with individuals, but to get into rapport with the group as a whole. To do this we need to sense where that group is, and it will not be going at the same speed as the individuals because those speeds are all different, the group itself forms its own identity. With a little reflection you can sense that and work with it not against it.

Rapport leaders

When matching and mirroring to a group, you can't possibly match and mirror every person individually or you'll look a bit weird! So simply pick out the rapport leaders in a room and match and mirror them. To find them (if it isn't already obvious) watch the ripples of movement in a room.

When one rapport leader moves, ripples of movement come from that central place (we all naturally match and mirror each other), so be observant to where the ripples originate from. Rapport leaders will change from time to time, so it's a good idea to be present to what's happening from moment to moment.

Practice Rapport with tough cases

As a practice, focus on the client or person in your life that you find hardest to get on with. Observe the timbre of their voice, is it high, or low, does it range a lot, or a little, does it grate on you, or is it mellifluous? What is the volume like, the speed of delivery?

Work on totally establishing rapport. Notice feelings of comfort and discomfort as they occur. Notice what is going on internally in your body as well as externally. Notice feelings as you go into rapport. After a few minutes you should notice the physiological feelings of rapport.

Also look for outward signs of rapport, which would be flushing of the face, dilation of pupils and a feeling of connection, like you've known them a long time. If you are not getting results, see your communication as inflexible rather than your clients being resistant.

In Greek mythology Procrustes had an iron bed onto which he invited guests to lie down. If the guest proved too tall, he would cut their legs to fit; if the guest was too short; he was stretched out on until he fitted. If we want to behave like Procrustes we can expect everyone else to fit our standard. However it would seem more sensible to try to adapt and maybe have a bed that can be more accommodating.

And in closing on the rapport section: With regard to all the techniques we're going to teach you in NLP, in terms of the intimate relationships that you'll be involved with, with all of your clients and your relationships, you need a foundation stone that's going to gain you trust.

This trust will give you time to have a conversation with them where you're going to get lots of facts, information about them. You're going to be reading their body language and noticing the patterns and beliefs they present to you. Having rapport gives you time and space, and this kind of agreement that you can be together and it's all right. It's the foundation of all of good NLP practise.

So you can even make a lot of mistakes yet with rapport and it doesn't matter. You can say the wrong thing and if you're in rapport it's OK. That's why it's so important. That's why it's the cornerstone of all your work.

Chapter 5
The Language of our realities - the representational system

In this chapter we look at

* how people's preferred representational system differs

* ways in which you can ascertain what representational system seems to dominate

* how you can use that information to become a more effective communicator

The language of life
We all have sensory preferences when we are communicating with others. For some time now the awareness in schools of the different learning styles of students has been gathering momentum. Ideally we all need things presented to us in a variety of ways to give learning the best possible chance to take place.

Although it's best to keep from classifying people in one way or another, from observing people's language, we can ascertain what their preferences are in which contexts.

Some prefer visual language, some prefer auditory, some very tactile, (kinaesthetic). A good communicator will tune in to the preferred communication style by taking note of the representational language and use that as a kind of dialect to enable enhanced communication.

This is easy to do once you have raised your awareness of the different styles and learnt how to speak the same inner dialect as others. You will be amazed at how much more easily you can get your message across and begin to see that everybody has their own personal way of experiencing their universe.

So how do we begin to recognize how each person makes sense of this unique world in which they live?

One of the easiest ways to discover this is to simply listen to the words that they're using. In NLP, we call this the VAKOG, (the representation system), which stands for visual, auditory, kinaesthetic, olfactory, and gustatory. The other system, which also plays a part in this, we call self-talk, the labelling system, or for short, Ai (audio internal).

According to NLP, for many practical purposes mental processing of events and memories can be treated as if performed by the five senses. For example, Einstein credited his discovery of spatial relativity to a mental visualization of "sitting on the end of a ray of light", but many people as part of decision-making talk to themselves in their heads and won't be making pictures at all.

The manner in which this is done, and the effectiveness of the mental strategy employed, plays a critical part in the way mental processing takes place. This observation led to the concept of a preferred representational system, the classification of people into fixed visual, auditory or kinaesthetic stereotypes.

This idea was later discredited and dropped within NLP by the early 1980's, in favour of the understanding that most people use all of their senses (whether consciously or unconsciously), and that whilst one system may seem to dominate, this is often contextualized - there is a balance that dynamically varies according to circumstance and mood.

NLP asserts that for most circumstances and most people, four of the five modes seem to dominate in mental processing:

* Visual thoughts - sight, mental imagery, spatial awareness
* Auditory - sound, speech, dialogue, quality of sounds
* Kinaesthetic (or feelings) sense - somatic feelings in the body, temperature, pressure, and also emotion.
* Self-talk (or audio internal)

The other two senses, gustatory (taste) and olfactory (smell), which are closely associated, often seem to be less significant in general mental processing, and are often considered jointly as one (possibly linked with feelings).

The preferred representational systems have been used for decades and many teachers have observed and believe that a student's modality (the words that they use to describe part of the VAKOG) strengths and weaknesses should be considered and that a student learns more when instruction is modified to match preferred modality patterns.

Michael Grinder (1991) has written about learning styles from the NLP point of view in his book Righting the Educational Conveyor Belt, giving instructions of how to make the diagnosis with NLP tools such as observing eye movements.

Research on VAKOG

Brockman (1980) experimented with counsellors. One cohort were asked to match representational systems (VAKOG) of their clients and the other counsellors took a more generic, human relations approach to empathising with their clients.

Results indicated that clients preferred the counsellor who matched representative systems by a ratio of 3 to 1 as opposed to the counsellors using more generic approaches. Although this is only one study, casual observation has indicated that this is an effective way to operate. If you apply the same findings to the teaching arena, it means that your pupils on a 3-1 ratio could find you more empathetic to some degree!

Representational systems are also relevant since some tasks are more optimally performed within one representational system than in another. For example, within education, spelling is better learned by clients who have unconsciously used a strategy of visualization, than an unconscious strategy of phonetically 'sounding out' (remember spelling strategies in chapter 2).

When taught to visualize, previously poor spellers can indeed be taught to improve. NLP proponents also found that pacing and leading the various cues tended to build rapport, and allowed people to communicate more effectively. Using similar representational systems to another person can help build rapport.

Skinner and Stephens (2003) explored the use of this model of representational systems in television marketing and communications - and this will be no surprise to many of you, just watch advertisements and notice how the advertising companies have discovered that using all the VAKOG in a short commercial will appeal to a wider audience than using just one or two.

A note here: Bearing in mind the notion that we are still to some degree in the arena of Rapport (matching and mirroring), the whole notion of energy still applies. It may not be the actual matching of representation systems that is happening here, but an inherent desire to communicate. Even so, the world is much more colourful when you can expand your awareness and find different ways to say the same thing!

Knowing which system you prefer to use over another can be useful.

Representational System Preference Test

For each of the following statements, please place a number next to every phrase. Use the following system to indicate your preferences:

4 = Closest to describing you
3 = Next best description
2 = Next best
1 = Least descriptive of you

1. I mostly make decisions about money based on:
_____the right gut level feelings
_____which is the best, sound solution and resonates for you
_____what looks best to me after clearly seeing the images
      in question
_____precise review and study of the situation

2. During an argument, I am most likely to be influenced by:
_____the loudness or softness of the other person's tone of
      voice

_____whether or not I can see the other person's viewpoint

_____the logic of the other person's argument

_____whether or not I am in touch with mine and the other person's feelings.

3. I like to be aware of the following in conversation:

_____the way people display themselves and give-away facial expressions

_____the feelings that we share

_____the words I and they choose and whether it all makes good sense

_____the variability of sounds and intonations in the 'story' of the voice

4. If I had the choice of these in order, first I would like to:

_____find the ideal volume and tuning on a stereo system

_____review the layout of the room to understand the person by this method

_____select the most comfortable furniture

_____look around and take in the décor, pictures and how the room looks before doing anything else.

5. Which describes your room that you live in:

_____the hi-fi is very prominent and you have an excellent CD/MP3 collection

_____it's a practical layout and things are situated in logical location

_____the feel of the place is the most important to you

_____the colours you choose and the way a room looks are most important

Step One: Copy your answers from the previous page to here

1.   K
            A
            V
            Ad

2.   A
            V
            Ad
            K

3.   V
            K
            Ad
            A

4.   A
            Ad
            K
            V

5.   A
            Ad
            K
            V

Step two: Add the numbers associated with each letter. There are 5 entries for each letter:

	V	A	K	AD
1				
2				
3				
4				
5				

This is a very simple and fun test and gives a generalized indication and by no means definitive. You would need to do more investigation to validate your results, like the exercise below.

Another way of finding out your preferences

If I was to give you the latest, state of the art DVD player with new features on it and it was your responsibility to make it work, would you:

A   Grab the manual and read it avidly

B   Take the articles out of the box and get to grips with it as you go

C   Talk to someone else about setting it up?

If you answered A, then that's your visual preference, B would be the tactile or kinaesthetic approach and C the auditory way. Again, these are not cast in stone, as they may change in differing contexts.

Chapter 6
Favoured Representational Systems

V: Visual

People who are visual often stand or sit with their heads and/or bodies erect, with their eyes up towards the ceiling. They will be breathing from the top of their lungs. They often sit very upright in their chair and tend to talk very quickly. They memorize by seeing pictures, and are less distracted by noise. Appearances are important to them. A visual person will be interested in how your lesson/program LOOKS.

A: Auditory

People who are auditory will move their eyes sideways. They breathe from the middle of their chest. They typically talk to themselves, and are easily distracted by noise, They will tend to spell phonetically. They prefer to learn something by hearing it. and usually like music and talking on the phone. The auditory person likes to be TOLD how they're doing, and responds to a certain tone of voice.   They will be interested in what you have to SAY about your program or how it SOUNDS to them.

K: Kinaesthetic

People who are kinaesthetic will typically be breathing

from the bottom of their lungs, They often move and talk verrry slooowly. They respond to physical rewards, and touching. They also may stand/sit closer to people than a visual person. They memorize by doing or walking through something. They will be interested in your program if it FEELS RIGHT.

Ai: Auditory Internal (self talk)
        I'm going to outline Ai in a lot more depth than the others
        as I know it's a harder notion to understand than the rest.

Firstly, let's start by outlining the different names this function has. Self-talk can be classified as Ai (auditory internal), AD (auditory digital), unclassified, the labelling system or simply the voice in your head. Phew glad we've got that understood. So, when you see all the names it has, just know it's that little voice that everyone has in their head that comments on everything!

As it's not a direct part of the hard wiring, I tend to work with it as a dissociated part of the representational system. That's not to say it's any less important to making changes within a learning system. In business, for instance, the labelling system is used more than any other representational system.

The Ai (or Ad) person will spend a fair amount of time talking to themselves. They will want to know if your program MAKES SENSE; is it logical, does it follow a structure etc? This auditory digital person can exhibit characteristics of the other major representational systems.

If you imagine being in the police force, with all the horrors you may encounter, you need to label fact as opposed to what you feel. Having AD as a primary representational system may be a very good idea. That way you don't have to experience the intensity through the other senses.

Self-talk is the habitual chatter that occupies your mind daily. If you are not too sure what I mean by that, just stop what you are doing and listen in: You have your own personal radio show going on inside your head!

This journalist in your head informs you of many things, yet has no real connection to reality as is known in fact. It relates to the filter systems (delete, distort, generalise) we were talking about in the early chapters.

When we worked with the presupposition *The Map is Not The Territory*, you may also see that the self-talk is also a map, not reality!

This voice in your head comments on everything yet has no power if not connected to the senses. With practice, you can gain control of the voice and make it yours again.

One technique I use with clients is to make the voice into another accent or at least make it a higher or lower pitch to distinguish it. That way, you begin to notice what are your chosen comments and what is a powerless (yet covertly influential) journalist.

It's a good thing to know that each individual likes their information in a certain way, whether they have good or bad experiences coupled with a certain VAKOG modality.

Some students can happily sit and listen for a long time, while others love to look at pictures to get good information. For some, neither of these learning styles will work. For those, they would have to try it out, use it, physically touch the subject, or even dance it!

This is well known in the corporate world, whereby the salesperson (if they have been well trained), will find out which modality is your favourite, and then sell to you in that way. If you were interested in a car for instance, and he/she finds out your favoured modality is tactile (kinaesthetic), they will get you to actually test drive the car!

Ideas for reflection

What have you learned about the different ways people represent their world? For instance, if a client tells you that they just can't grasp the information or that they don't feel good about a subject, what could you do for improved connection with them?

(A) If a person told you that they just can't stomach mathematics for instance, what representational system will they be using?

(B) If someone told you that they can't see the idea of physical exercise and that they just don't get the concept or structure of it, what modality are they in?

(The answers will be (A) K and (B) Ai.)

Categorisation of words in the Representational System

Using the tables below you can start to ascertain the preferred representational styles of anyone you have observed. The tables of words and phrases below give an idea of how to categorise words into representational systems. You may not agree with all of them, but you will see a pattern emerging as you read through. You may also feel more in tune with one column than others. Have a read through and find out.

Visual: Memorize by seeing pictures and are less distracted by noise. Often have trouble remembering and are bored by long verbal instructions because their mind may wander. They are interested in how the program **LOOKS**.

- See
- Look
- View
- Appear
- Show
- Dawn
- Reveal
- Envision
- Illuminate
- Imagine
- Clear
- Foggy
- Focused
- Hazy
- Crystal
- Picture

Auditory: Typically are easily distracted by noise. They can repeat things back to you easily & learn by listening. They like music and like to talk on the phone. Tone of voice and the words used can be important.

- Hear
- Listen
- Sound(s)
- Make music
- Harmonize
- Tune in/out
- Be all ears

- Rings a bell
- Silence
- Be heard
- Resonate
- Deaf
- Mellifluous
- Dissonance
- Question
- Unhearing

Kinaesthetic: Often they talk slowly. They respond to physical rewards & touching. They memorize by doing or walking through something.   They will be interested in a program that feels right or gives them a gut feeling.

- Feel
- Touch
- Grasp
- Get hold of
- Slip through
- Catch on
- Tap into
- Make contact
- Throw out
- Turn around
- Hard
- Unfeeling
- Concrete
- Scrape
- Get a handle
- Solid

Auditory Digital/Self Talk: They spend a fair amount of time talking to themselves. They memorize by steps, procedures, sequences. They will want to know the program makes sense. They can also sometimes exhibit characteristics of other rep systems.

- Understand
- Think
- Learn
- Process
- Decide
- Motivate
- Consider
- Change
- Perceive
- Insensitive
- Distinct
- Conceive
- Sense
- Structure
- Outline
- Condition

Translation between representational styles

Each of the representational 'languages' can be translated into the others. Look at the sentences below and see how differently the same situation can be matched using the same representational style, and how they can be described in different representational styles. Example 1. My future looks hazy

Match: Visual: When I look to the future, it doesn't seem clear.

Translate: Auditory: I can't tune in to my future.
                Kinaesthetic: I can't get a feel for what the future is
                holding for me.

Example 2. Sarah doesn't listen to me

Match: Auditory: Sarah goes deaf when I talk.
Translate: Visual: Sarah never sees me, even when I'm
                right in front of her eyes.
                Kinaesthetic: I get the feeling Sarah doesn't
                care to even try to catch my drift.

Example 3. Mary gets churned up inside when the head
           expects her assignment

Match: Kinaesthetic: Mary gets agitated and tense
                       over submitting her assignment.
Translate: Visual: Mary goes blind crazy and her
                       vision fogs up when her assignment
                       becomes due.
                       Auditory: Mary's ears ring because she
                       has to face the music if her assignment
                       isn't in on time.

Lead and Primary rep systems

In tricky situations where you need to determine someone's
strategies, knowing the difference between Lead representational
(rep) systems and Primary rep systems can be crucial.

The theory is that we have a lead rep system that kicks in every
time we go looking for information. We may have had this from

birth as it appears to be hard-wired to the extent that it's completely unconscious and is the go-getter for all information in any format. For instance, if a person has a lead system of visual, they use that modality to look for all other modalities.

The way you'd discover the lead representational system is to watch the eye patterns. If they flick up to visual every time you ask a question as the person is under pressure, you probably are looking at their lead rep system.

Why it's useful to know or distinguish is if you are looking for strategies by observing eye patterns. You'd get confused if you didn't know about lead and primary.

You detect lead systems via the eye patterns and physiology.

The primary representational system is how the person shows their inner world to the outside. This can be detected via physiology and the predicates they use.

Ideas to look at
Choose someone you work with and listen to the types of words they use. You will notice they will probably use all types of the visual, auditory and kinaesthetic words but one type will usually predominate. Then practice translating your language to their system.

If they say "I don't see what you mean," don't say "Let me repeat it," instead say "Let me *show you a different view.*" Then perhaps use an image or a pictorial example.

If they say "What you're saying doesn't feel right to me," don't say "Take a different view," instead say "Let's *move through* these points another way." Then use an example that means they have to move their body (or you, yours) to understand it.

Keep practicing and make a note of what you have done to reinforce your learning. You will become more and more aware of how other people think, and more flexible in how you respond.

Remember to employ all of your NLP skills you have read about and practiced – build rapport, mirror, get the trust of the parent, whatever it takes to get into their world.

To summarise
When people are like each other they like each other.

When you like someone, you are willing to assist them get what they want. Most communication is outside our conscious awareness.

As a master communicator you will communicate best with people when you employ their preferred ways of speaking. If you are working with someone who is in high visual sit up in your chair, breath from the top of your lungs – within reason!

If you are with someone who is auditory, slow down a bit, modulate your voice more and listen, really listen.

If they are kinaesthetic, slow waaaay doooown. Talk to them about feelings. Change your pace so that it matches theirs, and really get a feel for what they are communicating.

You will know when you are in rapport, you will feel congruent, movements will mirror and match – you can begin to lead and they will follow your movements, you may feel a sense of warmth and they may feel they have known you all their life.

Chapter 7
Presuppositions in Language

NLP has a huge following, and a lot has to do with the fantastic approach and work inside language patterns.

As a human race, we tend to be used by language rather than using it. NLP has put us back in the driving seat again by giving us a way to understand language and use it consciously.

When I mention language, I am not just talking about presentation skills or how we outwardly use NLP skills in talking; I am moving you into a dynamic that is beyond words, the very fabric of creation itself, before the spoken word.

Originally, before most records were re-written, language was mostly verbs without nouns. There were not even many spaces between words, like a huge code.

When our brains began to enlarge, we got a huge library and had to begin to live more from the past, from our history, and more from nouns than verbs.

With the advent of language (used in the past historical sense), we actually invented problems that existed through language itself. We literally imprisoned ourselves in walls of linguistic history that has been a challenge to permeate. A little like the story of Arthur and The Stone (spirit or energy trapped inside matter).

To give you an example, when you have some personal events that happen to you in your life and you make a decision about those events, your senses will start to project a virtual world in front of you, and increase your internal evidence of the decision you made up. Of course, you will be right about the decision and have masses of proof all around you, but the problem is, the decision was already past based; it's not absolutely true!

The only way out of this self-inflicted prison of linguistic glue is to be able to get inside the events and reframe them, therefore releasing the language that held them together. Sometimes time can do this itself with some passive witnessing of the events, yet NLP has evolved some very graceful techniques to get inside these patterns easily and quickly.

On the NLP Practitioner we give you the basics for doing this and then add to your mastery on our Master Practitioner Course. On the NLP Master Practitioner course you will find an incredible recourse of linguistic tools, including advanced presuppositions in language leading into Quantum Linguistics.

If you have watched movies like *What The Bleep* or read books such as *The Holographic Universe*, you are already on the way to understanding the beyond logic approach to life.

We live in a world of perceptions (Plato called the world we live in, the world of illusions); the nature of this world is governed by how we thread sentences together to literally create our lives in thought forms. This is where the word spelling came from. It meant your ability to cast spells; spell-ing. The Egyptians knew these secrets and knew the power of language when harnessed and used properly.

As you may imagine, this "quantum field" is an exciting place to travel to: It's a place beyond words, and therefore beyond problems.

So how does one get into the quantum field and then how do you use it via language?

Below is a set of ways of using presuppositions in language. If you can remember that each presupposition (existence, awareness etc.) is part of the glue that makes up reality, you'll be able to follow why they are so effective:

What assumption do you have to accept for each?

1.   Existence —Basically everything has existence in it; so what would you like to bring into existence in the listener? Also saying 'not' does not change the thing you want the person to listen to internally.

a.   I didn't *realise how powerful NLP* is
b.   Our clients are the ones who tell us that *our products are excellent*
c.   The *happiness of people* rains down on us

2.   Possibility/Necessity- These lead your nervous system, guiding it into possibilities it didn't see, or shepherding it by putting 'pressure' on via bullying language such as 'have to', 'should' and 'must'.

a.   In business you have to know that techniques like *NLP can* make a huge difference to your ability to expand your company. Can you know that to *be possible* now?

b.   I realised I *can integrate NLP* into work easily

c.   Our clients *can realise* that what we do always *has to be* excellent

d.   Just because you've *been able* to cope doesn't mean you *have to* just cope

3.   Cause – Effect – A makes B – People put two things together by linking cause to one or other component. This linkage is arbitrary and can be utilised to link any one idea with another to sound plausible.

a.   Don't sit in that chair unless you're prepared *to make the decision*

b.   Studying NLP *will make you* money

c.   *It was the marketing* we did that *made our clients* buy from us

d.   The rainy summer *led to the poor performance* this year

e.   Only investment in the *future creates results* now

f.   *Because* you're not getting what you currently want, *it's time do something about it*

4.   Complex Equivalence – means – A & B at the same time – In the same family as cause and effect. With these patterns there is no time involved before any linkage. Literally THIS equals THIS

a.   *Just because you're asking* those questions *means you're* already interested in my propositions

b.   You being short of *time means you* need to invest in working smarter

c.   The fact that there's a recession on *means that selling* is difficult

d.   The fact that we advertise in the national press *means we* are well recognised as a market leader

e.   Being a businessman *means you understand* the need to invest

5.   Awareness – VAKOG – Anything that involves the senses

a.   Now you can *see the excellent* value of this product
b.   Because you've *heard just how* this will work for you, now can you be *aware of all* the new possibilities?
c.   Can you *taste the* sweet smell of success?
d.   Now you know all about presuppositions how *are you seeing* yourself using them?

6.   Time – Used proficiently, time is a graceful way to make changes

a.   It *has been* a real problem not being able to do those things that you wanted to do, *now* that can see how those new solutions will have come into your business so that you can know how easy it is to get the results you want *right now*
b.   Our last client didn't realise the impact NLP would have on her team until she *saw the future* of the changes all happening *right now*
c.   Once you have reached an understanding of how much this has *cost you in the past*, you will *know now* how your decision to *go forward* with this is *recreating your future*
d.   Projections show that *past performance* never match *current capabilities*

7.   Adverb/Adjective - Presuppose that something is going to happen. The issue is how will the experience be?

a.   Things need to move *quickly* to ensure we get the best results

b.   Our successful clients know how *easy* it is to get results

c.   Making big changes *easily* is our speciality

d.   *Slow* incremental changes are a belief of the past.

8.   Exclusive/Inclusive Or – excludes something – DIGITAL A or B, includes everything ANALOGUE A or something else – gives illusion of choice, Erickson – "I think my clients ought to have the illusion of choice whilst they do exactly as I say"

a.   I think my clients ought to have at least three choices to ponder *whilst they* implement the changes I want them to.

b.   Exclusive - John couldn't decide whether to climb the mountain *now or at 7am* the next day (= going to climb the mountain)

c.   Inclusive – would you like the *red or blue* phone?

d.   Would you like *alloy wheels or the normal ones*?

e.   Would you like us to *invoice you now or after* your financial year end?

f.   Pay by *cash or cheque*?

g.   Would you like the appointment *Monday or Tuesday*? (Don't ask them "would you like an appointment?")

9.   Ordinal – A list of things that if not completed in the right order would fail the objective.

a.   The *second thing* you need to know about ordinal presuppositions is even more important than the first

b.   There are *three things* that are important here. Firstly that you understand the presuppositions unconsciously and second you able to use them whenever the time is right.

c.   Whatever decision *you make next* will be the one to change your results

Chapter 8
Hierarchy of ideas (or chunking up and down)

The Hierarchy of ideas: A linguistic tool that allows the speaker to traverse the realms of abstract to specific easily and effortlessly.

Computer programmers are used to moving easily up and down levels of abstraction. A directory is made up of files. Each file may have many records, each record many fields, each field many bytes. Expressions give rise to statements, grouped into functions, libraries, and then applications.

The ability to operate over so many levels of abstraction is arguably one of the traits that make us human. Managers who can move up and down levels of abstraction will be able to use this skill easily and effectively in dealing with people, even those who are not programmers, provided they understand some simple principles.

As we get more and more abstract, we deal with larger and larger chunks of data. As we get more concrete, we deal with smaller and smaller chunks of data. Imagine a hierarchy of ideas or concepts with the most abstract and all-embracing at the top and the most concrete at the bottom. When we 'chunk up', we move up the hierarchy of ideas. When we 'chunk down.' we get more and more concrete.

So, starting with a person, John, we might chunk up to see John as a male, then as an Englishman, then as human, then as a living entity. Or we might chunk down from John and examine his face, and then his eyes, and then his left retina, then a single cell in the retina, and so on.

Chunking is a good concept for a manager to understand, because many communication difficulties involve mismatched chunk sizes. John may use smaller chunks than Adam and see Adam as vague and kind of sleep-inducing when he talks. Adam may see John as terribly boring and caught up in detail. In meetings, Sarah may get 'picky' and slow the meeting down.

As a manager, you probably need to process bigger chunks than your employees and smaller chunks than your manager. Ideally, your employees will learn that you don't want to hear all the details of their jobs, and you will learn the same about your manager.

It is useful to be able to 'chunk up' and 'chunk down' when you need to improve communication. When talking to someone using bigger chunks, you can ask the question, "What, specifically?" to get more details. When talking to someone using smaller chunks, you can ask, "What is the intention of this?" Or "What is this an instance of?" to encourage larger chunks.

There are many ways to chunk up and chunk down. Frequently, you can get a meeting or discussion back on track by chunking up and then chunking down a different way. We tend to differ less on the bigger-chunk items. Most people in a meeting could agree on such sweeping statements, such as "We want the company to succeed." So when there is disagreement, chunking up to a place where

THE HIERARCHY OF IDEAS

people agree can help to defuse the tension and give everyone more context. You can then carefully chunk down, preserving agreement, to develop the details that you need to.

You may have heard that language can be, at one extreme, vague and general and, at the other, very specific. Language is the best way we have to communicate, but it is often extremely limited. By understanding the limitations of language you can get a great deal more from it than by remaining in ignorance.

Between the general and the vague, and the detailed and specific, there are a number of gradations expressing things more or less generally or specifically. Certain words have a hypnotic effect because they cause us to search around in our minds trying to find some meaning, which is often difficult or impossible.

To start with it is better to take an example of a word such as 'furniture'. With a great deal of agreement, we can show the levels of generality in the example below.

The word 'furniture' is a general word. An armchair is also a general word, but it is more specific than furniture. On this continuum from general to specific, there are seats and chairs which come in the middle - they are more specific than furniture and more general than armchair.

Under the category of seats we have chairs, settees and stools as examples of seats. These items are on the same level and additional examples of seats. Also, under chairs we have armchair and dining chair, which are examples of chairs and are on the same level of general.

We take information in chunks (often 5 to 9 chunks), which is why being able to traverse abstract to specific should increase your pay packet. A general idea is a big chunk because it contains a lot of information and refers to many items. And a more specific word is a smaller chunk because it contains fewer examples.

When we chunk up we become more general. When we chunk down we become more specific. And when we chunk across, we keep at the same level of generality. So from a chair, we can chunk up to a seat. And from a chair we can chunk down to armchairs. We can chunk across from a chair to a stool.

We can chunk up by asking either:
What is the purpose of a chair? (Seating, balance.)
Or - What is the intention of a chair? (Seating, comfort.)

Chunking down
We can chunk down by asking:
What is an example of (a chair)? (Stool, armchair.)
For instance? (Same.)
What specifically makes a chair?

Chunking across
We can chunk across by asking:
What's are other examples of seating? (Fairground rides, upturned milk crates.)

Illustrative conversation
She: "What shall we do tonight?"
He: "What about going to the cinema?" (This is an example of doing things, chunking down.)
She: "Well, if you'd like that form of entertainment, I'd rather go to the opera." (This is an example of chunking up to entertainment from cinema, then chunking across to opera.)
He: "You prefer something classy & arty?" (Chunks up from opera to arty, which is one example of something more abstract/general

than opera.)

She: "Yes".

He: "What about the ballet?" (Chunks down from classy & arty to ballet, which is an example of arty.)

She: "Good idea, I'll get the popcorn." (That's a chunking down joke)!

So we can see that just in the use of simple linguistics, we can move/ traverse from the very abstract to the ultra specific to gain rapport with as many other 'universes' out there called people! Let's now see how this relates to working one on one with clients: When a client comes to see me, I immediately chunk up on their situation.

If they say they are lowly, not worth a penny and useless, I see through that to something else. I'm thinking to myself, if a person is that useless, why would they spend good money and time on me?

Also they must have some pretty high intention to be here in the first place!

There is no situation where you have to take a low level behaviour and be stuck with seeing just that view forever. So the trick with using chunking to good effect with clients is to always separate the intention from the behaviour.

The intention will always be a high level value, one that we all can relate to. The behaviour will be the low level physical representation of them not achieving the intention! So, whilst holding the gross. low level physical reality, also be able to chunk up to a place that describes what their intention may well be towards.

Just below, we have a template version of chunking up and down, using a car as an example.

Abstract languaging - Creates trance effect
{Intuitor Big Picture, Abstract—Milton Model}

Existence
Movement
Transportation

Chunk Up ("For what purpose/Intention"?)
Ford Capri GT
Chunk Across ("What are other examples"?)

Buses -- Boats -- Cars -- Planes – Trains

Chunk Down ("What specifically"?)
Classes & Categories Parts
Bodywork
Engine
Wheels
Hub Caps
Wheel Nuts

The Structure of Nit-Picking: Chunking Down and
Mismatching Specific — Meta Model/ Details/Sensor
Specific - Out of Trance

Lateral thinking

The process of lateral thinking comes about when you chunk up, then chunk down to another meaning or context or object. For example (see next page also), a Ford Capri, for what purpose? (Chunking up question). For transportation; what are other forms of transportation? Bus!! There we have it, a simple lateral movement.

When you come onto the Metaphor section (chapter 9), you'll notice that the whole premise of making a good metaphor is your ability to chunk up and then down to another place - laterally moving the client to different thinking.

Chapter 9
Metaphors

Some years ago, whilst running a class for Swedish Clients delivering information about metaphors, I was asked by a student, "what exactly is a metaphor?" I answered that it was just like a story but has very influential pieces to it. "Why don't you just call it a story then?" Was the retort I got back. After consideration, I decided not to answer her question directly, or challenge the challenge, so I told her this:

Just imagine, in times before newspapers, television, Internet or any kind of expanded communication systems, other ways had to be evolved to allow people to know what's going on in the world. When you tune in to the way they did this, it was in the form of poem, plays and songs. Inside these forms was all the information you may need.

We are all very familiar with the use of metaphor, we all know that a metaphor is the use of words or phrases to directly compare a seemingly unrelated thing, the Compact Oxford English dictionary defines it thus: 'A figure of speech in which a word or phrase is applied to something to which it is not literally applicable (e.g. food for thought) or a thing symbolic of something else.'

The term metaphor originally comes from Greek metaphora (meta, meaning 'over', and herein, 'to carry'). This transfer (or carry) of meaning within all cultures and languages has a long history of use as evidenced in the teaching of Aristotle and Plato.

Lakoff and Johnson (1980) have this to say about metaphor:

'In all aspects of life...we define our reality in terms of metaphors and then proceed to act on the basis of the metaphors. We draw inferences, set goals, make commitments, and execute plans, all on the basis of how we in part structure our experience, consciously and unconsciously, by means of metaphor.' (p 158)

Parables and allegories use language metaphorically, and again here you can see how great communicators of the past have used metaphor to excellent effect – Jesus, Ghandi, Socrates, Descartes. More modern examples are Winston Churchill, J F Kennedy, Nelson Mandela. A simple leap then can take us into the training room or one to one with clients and we see how useful metaphor can be.

In training we use metaphor through story, poetry, art all of the time. But are we sufficiently aware about what we are doing? In this part of the chapter we intend to encourage you to raise that awareness so that you can switch into metaphor mode more easily and illustrate how metaphor can be used with change techniques to enhance success.

Metaphor works on the conscious and unconscious mind simultaneously, the conscious mind being concerned with the details of the story or 'face value' while the unconscious mind will process the symbolic meanings and make the learning transferable to other situations. We can embed messages that are barely detectable to the listener or reader into the stories we tell. You may have noticed that politicians and advertisers are doing this all the time!

We all have our own story and we change this story as we travel through life. The story may seem recognisable to someone who knows us well, but it is nonetheless a metaphor of our life. If you are to bear in mind the map is not the territory – in the same way your life story is not your life (it just appears that way)! we can change the way we see our lives through the story we write about it and in this way change the way we approach life, for the better.

From personal experience, metaphors are the most powerful ways of getting information across that I have found. Different uses of metaphor reflect people's sociocultural constructions of the world and can indicate what is significant in a particular culture and what is personally significant to those who create metaphors. Many have argued that metaphors make us, rather than us making metaphors (Stacey, 1997) and this influence may have more significance than we realise for our development.

Think back to the special stories that have influenced you in your life and notice why. What happened inside you when you hear/heard these metaphors?

What Metaphors do

Metaphors in particular can be effective and powerful learning tools when used consciously.

They can:

- link abstracts to concrete language
- ignite the mind to multi-levels of understanding
- give understanding about the ways your learners view their

internal 'map'
- help & aid memory for all clients by creating associations or links
- train & help learners to make sense of information and issues
- uplift & facilitate unspoken or unconscious learning
- promote and encourage emotions.
.

You can use them as a device to facilitate unconscious integration of work you are doing or have done with a client: Metaphors allow clients to explore their feelings in a safe, non-judgmental way and to clarify emotions by using revealing images or comparisons.

Metaphors in the mix

Metaphors are wonderful indicators of the sense a person favours. To begin with, you can ask a person to give you an indication, through metaphor of their internal experience.

Ask them something like this:

'When you're learning, what is that learning like?' You are looking for sensory data. Here's an example of what you encouraging.

Learning is.....

Painting a picture that takes shape over time
Wading through mud!
Eating something really hard to chew that stays in your mouth for ages and then you don't know how to get rid of it
A long, long journey that I eventually paid a ticket for
Being in the dark for ages then a light comes on and I can work it out

When you get into your clients world, you can then start to develop metaphors appropriately to the very deepest recesses of their storage cupboards.

Using metaphor for the conscious and unconscious mind:

There are two ways of utilizing metaphor: One is to the conscious mind, the other the unconscious.

When using metaphors for the conscious mind, your client will know what you are talking about and will be able to follow the trail fairly easily. If the metaphor is skilfully constructed, the follower will need to exercise their minds at least a little.

Metaphors require the brain to do a little gymnastics to be able to understand the meaning the speaker is trying to convey and sometimes, when the metaphor is understood, the meaning will be far deeper than if simple literal language were used. This is why poetry can be so meaningful and evocative in so few words.

Using a narrative approach to overcoming behaviour problems:
Using metaphor encourages the externalisation of thoughts and feelings. In work with clients with ADHD one of the techniques that has been used is to encourage the student to give their behaviour a name, so working with Mikel, he called his ADHD behaviour 'the Abdabs' he was then able to distinguish between himself – Mikel- as a person and the behaviour as the Abdabs.

Once this distinction existed, it was possible for Mikel to engage in a challenge to see how much of each day had 'the Abdabs' been in control and how much of the day had Mikel been in control. This technique can be used with many other emotions like anger, anxiety, shyness, and so on.

Multi-sensory Imagination

Don't forget to use lots of multi-sensory language when providing activities for your learners. Consider what sort of language you are using to evoke a response, remembering we all have slightly differing styles of learning. To evoke a multi-sensory response, ask multi-sensory questions:

Kinaesthetic imagination: 'Imagine being in a field of long, lush grass. How would that feel? How might you act in this field right now?

Visualisation: 'Can you imagine what that would look like?'
Auditory imagination: 'In this field, what sounds are there, what do these sounds remind you of? Imagine a storyteller beginning a story here: You can hear the story and its details...what would it sound like?'

Then you can layer in some of the concepts you'd like to get across, using fields, grass, clouds, wind, water or anything that will represent the problem.... and solution!

Case study on the use of metaphor

You never know how much difference a metaphor can make in someone's life!

I was asked to talk to a 6 year old girl, Megan, by her mother. Megan had contracted Asthma three years previously and her mother knew how I used metaphor to hear and speak effectively with kids and adults.
I used a toy to talk through with her to find out about whatever was happening in Megan's life and it went well. She could talk much more freely when she was talking through a rabbit and the rabbit knew things that Megan didn't, even if the rabbit was herself!

After this "talk" we had, she seemed satisfied with what we had discovered about some undisclosed "truths" in her life, but then turned to me and asked me a question that rooted me to the spot. She put her head in her hands and said to me "I just wish I knew more about what life is all about…"

Just imagine the responsibility I felt at that time. I stood there, with a thousand thoughts whirring around amuck inside my mind. I looked through the window and let providence guide me. As I saw the flowers and plants waving gently in the wind, something came to me that would let us both describe a new world of learning about life (and make me feel relieved I found the 'right' metaphor).

"See that plant outside Megan?", I said. "Yes," she replied curiously. "Well as you watch that plant grow, it would start from just a seed. Inside that seed had all the knowledge for its whole lifetime of growth. It doesn't know what flower it will be all at once, but all the information for the plant is in the seed, so the plant will always know what to do, but only one leaf at a time."

She was totally pleased with her metaphor and hurried back to life once more, not encumbered by her past issues.

Before that day Megan had Asthma every year for the previous three years. Her Asthma desisted for the next three years (while her good friend still had her own Asthma problem) and never came back to this day as far as I know.

So am I saying that metaphor cures illnesses? Well, no and yes; yet the proof is evident of how they get messages across effectively and deeply.

Another metaphor (perhaps not a true story yet still good for instruction) that struck me as perfect for teaching or training was this:

I was returning from school one day and I saw a dog with a collar on in my garden. I had a short piece of string in my bag, so I went to the dog and placed the string around its collar. I somehow knew the dog would head off in the right direction, yet I didn't know what the right direction was. Now and then he would forget he was on the pavement and start into a field.

So I would pull on him a bit and call his attention to the fact the pavement was where he was supposed to be. And finally, about four miles from where I had boarded him, he turned into a farmyard and the farmer said, "So the runaway has come back. Where did you find him?" I said, "About four miles from here." "How did you know you should come here?" I said, "I didn't know. The dog knew. All I did was keep his attention on the road".

The last metaphor has several different slants, yet you can see its value in defining a client/practitioner relationship.

One of my favourite metaphors talks about commitment:

There was a time as boys and as men when caps were an important part of life. You may have had as few caps as two in your whole life! When the boys used to run through fields and came across a wall or obstacle that they couldn't climb easily, they'd throw their caps over the obstacle. That way they knew they would make sure they'd have to climb it!

Deeper, unconscious metaphor

The metaphors above are fairly easy to understand and are of the conscious kind. What about deeper metaphor that the conscious mind has no understanding of at all?

The Boiler Factory

This metaphor has been adapted from an original by Milton Erickson

We learn things in a very unusual way, a way that we don't know about. Milton Erickson was always a very curious man. Even after 60 years in his profession, he never purported to know everything about his clients. In fact he got really curious about what makes them tick, what excites them, what values they have.

In my first year of college I happened to come across, that summer, a boiler factory. The crews were working on twelve boilers at the same time, and it was three shifts of workmen. And those pneumatic hammers were pounding away, driving rivets into the boilers. I heard that noise and I wanted to find out what it was. On learning that it was a boiler factory, I went in and I couldn't hear anybody talking. I could see the various employees were conversing. I could see the foreman's lips moving, but I couldn't hear what he said to me. He heard what I said. I had him come outside so I could talk to him. And I asked him for permission to roll up in my blanket and sleep on the floor for one night.

He thought there was something wrong with me. I explained that I was a premedic student and that I was interested in learning processes. And he agreed that I could roll up in my blanket and sleep on the floor. He explained to all the men and left an explanation for the succeeding shift of men. The next morning I awakened. I could hear the workmen talking about that damn fool kid. What in hell was he sleeping on the floor there for? What did he think he could learn?

During my sleep that night I blotted out all that horrible noise of the twelve or more pneumatic hammers and I could hear voices. I knew that it was possible to learn to hear only certain sounds if you tune your ears properly.

There you have the relationship between conscious and unconscious communication, with enough instruction to the unconscious about what to do and how to do it, plus enough communication to the conscious mind to keep it satisfied along the journey

"So what is a metaphor?" I was asked back in Sweden. And why didn't I call them just stories?

Perhaps you can now see for yourselves that a metaphor can carry the narrative, emotion, pictures, sounds, feelings and thinking that connect with the inner minds of each speaker and listener. You could say that a metaphor will "carry" a story.

Personally, I like to read many metaphors, learn a few and see the way they are put together, then let myself start constructing them, trusting the deeper part of my brain to bring the plan together.

Think of a time in the past when you used metaphor naturally to good effect with another person, either at home or at work. Now see if you can augment the metaphor consciously to suit another situation aside from the original one.

How to design metaphors:

For those of you that like process and structure, here's a method of designing metaphors. As said earlier, I trust my mind to make them up for me - if you need more structure the next part is for you.

The major purpose of a metaphor is to pace and lead a client's behaviour through a story. The major points of construction consist of:

(A) Displacing the referential index from the client to a character in a story

(B) Pacing the person's problem by establishing behaviours and events between the characters in the story that are similar to those in the person's situation

(C) Accessing resources for the person within the context of the story

(D) Finishing the story such that a sequence of events occurs in which the characters in the story resolve the conflict and achieve the desired outcome.

The basic steps to generate a metaphor are as follows;

Premapping

1.   Identify the sequence of behaviour and/or events in question: This could range from a conflict between internal parts, to a physical illness, to problematic interrelationships between the client and parents, a boss or a spouse.

2.   Strategy analysis: Is there any consistent sequence of representations contributing to the current behavioural outcome?

3.   Identify the desired new outcomes and choices: This may be done at any level of detail, and is important that you have an outcome to work for.

4.   Establish anchors for strategic elements involved in this current behaviour and the desired outcome. For instance, in one knee you might anchor all of the strategies and representations that stop the person from having the necessary choices; and on the other knee you might anchor any personal resources (regardless of specific contexts) that the person may have.

5.   Displace referential indices: Map over all nouns (objects and elements) to establish the characters in the story. The characters may be anything, animate or inanimate, from rocks to forest creatures to cowboys to books, etc. What you choose as characters is not important so long as you preserve the character relationship. Very often you may want to use characters from well-known fairy tales and myths.

6.   Establish an isomorphism between the persons situation and behaviour, and the situation and behaviours of the characters in the story - map over all verbs (relations and interactions):
Assign behavioural traits, such as strategies and representational characteristics, that parallel those in the client's present situation (i.e. pace the person's situation with the story). Make use of any anchors you have established previously to secure the relationship.

7.   Access and establish new resources in terms of the characters and events in the story: This may be done within the framework of a Reframing or re-accessing of a forgotten resource; again, using any appropriate pre-established anchors. You may choose to keep the actual content of the resource ambiguous allowing the persons unconscious processes to choose the appropriate one.

8.   Use non sequiturs, ambiguities and direct quotes to break up sequences in the story and direct conscious resistance, if such

resistance is present and is hindering the effect of the metaphor. Conscious understanding does not, of course, necessarily interfere with the metaphoric process.

9.   Keep your resolution as ambiguous as necessary to allow the person's unconscious processes to make the appropriate changes. Collapse the pre-established anchors and provide a future pace, if possible, to check your work.

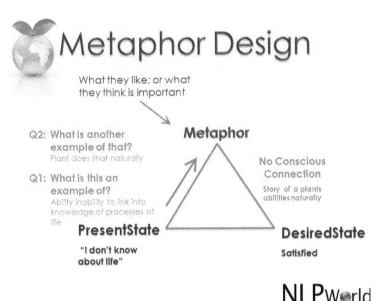

Metaphor Design

What they like; or what they think is important

Q2: What is another example of that?
Plant does that naturally

Q1: What is this an example of?
Ability inability to link into knowledge of processes of life

Metaphor

No Conscious Connection
Story of a plants abilities naturally

PresentState
"I don't know about life"

DesiredState
Satisfied

NLPWorld

Summary:

Metaphors have educational uses beyond the cognitive and literary. They can provide poignant insights and enhance emotional development. The unconscious mind has a language of its own. With metaphor we can communicate with an unconscious mind to turn on a light and process information that may have been filtered out via the gatekeepers of the conscious mind.

Chapter 10
The Milton Model

Milton Erickson was generally regarded as the foremost hypnotherapist of his time. He worked with trance and cleverly structured sentences full of vague meanings to help his clients discover how to address their problems and the resources that they already had available to them.

Erickson's success was based on his ability to read non-verbal behaviour (sensory acuity), his ability to establish rapport with his clients, his skill with language patterns and his beliefs about his clients. Some of his beliefs appear in the list of NLP Presuppositions. For example:

Every behaviour has a positive intention. This is the best choice available to a person given the circumstances as they see it. Respect for the other person's model of the world. Resistance in a client is due to a lack of rapport. That is, there are no resistant clients, only inflexible therapists.

Erickson would also pace a client's experience and then begin to lead them into trance (or downtime). In NLP terms, uptime is when your senses are focused on the outside world, while downtime is related to your inner being. The Meta Model is associated with uptime (i.e. who, what, how specifically), while the Milton Model is associated with downtime. As we go through our daily activities, we are continually cycling through uptime and downtime and are often somewhere in-between.

The Milton Model hypnotic language patterns encourage the listener to move away from detail and content and move to higher levels of thinking and deeper states/complexities of mind. Some patterns are used to establish a trance state (or downtime/relaxation in the body). Other patterns are used to loosen the listener's model of the world from which he is expressing his current behaviours and to consider a more expansive interpretation of what is possible.

For the Milton Model, we use some of the same language patterns, but this time we wish to be vague so that the client can easily go into trance and/or from the vague suggestions choose a suggested course of action that will address his problem/issue.

Pacing and Leading

To pace a client, begin by matching and mirroring her physiology, choice of words, tone of voice, etc., then make reference to what she would most likely be seeing, hearing, feeling or thinking (e.g. "As you notice the lights slowly dimming ..." or "As you hear my voice ..." or As you feel the chair on your back ...", or "As you wonder ...") while speaking slowly in a soft tonally and pacing your speech to her breathing. To lead her into downtime, you would begin to focus her attention inward by saying something such as "You may notice how easy it is to close your eyes whenever you wish to feel more relaxed ..."

The topic of trance and hypnosis is vast. The rest of this article will focus on the Milton Model Patterns, which is a set of language patterns used to:

1)   Pace and lead
2)   Distract the conscious mind
3)   Speak directly to the unconscious and access its hidden
        resources

Below are some examples of how to use what we call the Milton
Model. You can then adapt them to suit your own context of working
with clients or for business purposes.

The Milton Model Patterns:

1. **Mind Read:** Claiming to know another's thoughts or feelings
without specifying the how you came to that knowledge.
"I know that you believe ..." or "I know you're thinking ..."
"I know you are wondering how much you will learn from this
training."
"You may be curious about how you will use these patterns."
We must be cautious to keep our references as general as possible. If
specific details clash with the listener's thoughts, it will disrupt his
or her attention.

2. **Lost Performative:** Expressing value judgments without
identifying the one doing the judging.
It's important to know about these structures, because it's often
necessary to deliver presuppositions indirectly. These types of
phrases contain at least one judgment or evaluation of which we
can't identify the source.
"It's important to learn language patterns."
"It's essential to have fun learning all this stuff."
"It's good that we are all here tonight."
The speaker doesn't state exactly who thinks these things are good,
necessary or important. "Breathing is good."

3. **Cause & Effect:** Implies one thing leads to or causes another; that there is sequence of cause/effect and a flow in time. Includes phrases such as: "If ..., then ...; As you ...., then you ...; Because ... then ..."

"If you can listen well, *then you can* learn many things."

"The occasional sounds and noises from outside *make you more determined* to get what's here." Here you have words like makes, causes, forces, because and requires.

A linkage works by connecting a statement that is pacing something that is already occurring with a statement that leads the listener to some other (usually internal) experience.

Conversely, many people put together life-sentences that trap them. My knees hurt....*that's because* I'm getting old." Part of your job is to recognise these and then dissolve these life-sentences.

4. **Complex Equivalence:** Attributes meaning to something that may or may not have a 'cause' capability. *This* means *This*.

"Being here means that you will change easily."

"As soon as she saw his face she knew she loved him."

"Working with NLP World means results."

5. **Presupposition:** The linguistic equivalent of assumptions. These are ways of indirectly getting agreement from a listener. There are several types of presuppositions:

a) **Existence:** "She saw the ice cream in the freezer." Implies is, was, may be. "John didn't see a goat behind a tree." Well what do we now know that John doesn't?

b) **Time:** Before, after, during, continue, yet, already, begin, stop, start, still, while, since, as, and when. "You may hear noises in the room while you are entering a state of deep relaxation."

c) **Ordinals:** These assume action will be taken, the question is, in what order, 1st, 2nd, 3rd, etc. "Do you want to take a deep breath or would you like to settle down into your chair first?"

d) **Ors:** "Would you prefer a silk blouse or one in cotton?" This presupposes that the listener wants one of them. The question is which? It's better than asking "do you want one?" Of which it can be easy to answer "no!"

e) **Awareness:** These assume the statement is true, all that may be questioned is whether the listener is aware. "Have you realized how common it is to be in a trance?" "Have you noticed how often you go into a trance, even by yourself?"

f) **Adverbs and Adjectives:** Presuppose that something is going to happen. The issue is how will the experience be?
"What have you *enjoyed* the most about driving the new RX-7?"
"Are you *excited* about making this purchase?"
"How *easily* can you begin to relax?"
"Fortunately we have *plenty* of opportunity to practice this material."
"Will you be *changing* your attitude now or later today?" It is assumed the person will change their attitude, the only unknown is when.

6. **Universal Quantifier:** Universal generalizations without referential index.
"Everyone; No one; All; Every"
"*Everyone* knows the fears of the people of London." Do they!!?
"We *all* respect the elders." "*All* upstanding people pay their taxes."
These patterns are used to demand authority of the speaker or writer. They try and manipulate the listener into believing the person via utilizing groups of people (who are not actually there).

7. **Modal Operator:** Words that refer to possibility or necessity or that reflect internal states of intensity tied to our rules in life. They can be used to direct the listener's experience in a certain direction.

"How fortunate you are *to be able* to learn so easily. It *can* happen when the student is really ready to know how quickly it *will* happen." "You *should* care for others." Or "You *must* resolve this issue."

8. **Nominalization:** Words which are formed as nouns and which are shorthand for processes.

"People can come to *new understandings.*" Here 'understandings' is used as a noun and is shorthand to describe the on-going experience of 'understanding' or 'making sense of something.'
If I were to say, "you know that you can feel confident about some *learnings* from last weekend," it is much easier for you to agree than If I was to say "you know that you can feel confident about unspecified noun structures from last weekend . . . "

The word 'Learnings' is an example of a nominalisation. To nominalise something means to make a noun out of something intangible, which doesn't exist in a concrete sense (in NLP, we say any noun that you can't put in a wheelbarrow is a nominalisation). In this example, the process of learning something is turned into a noun, *learnings*. When we 'rubber stamp' an area and make it solid, we literally can kill the process and make the moving, the stopped!

Being unwell becomes a disease. (Note that dis-ease once was a process of not at ease).
Being depressed becomes depression.
A state like depression becomes an enormous and sometimes insurmountable, overwhelming state of being; for example, whereas being depressed to most people is more likely to imply a state that

has a beginning, and more importantly an end. A block is something much more insurmountable than something that is merely blocking your progress.

"So close your eyes and think for a moment about some recent learning, one that may have given you much surprise and enjoyment." Notice in the previous sentence the speaker doesn't say how or where, but allows the listener to fill in with his or her own details.

9. **The More:** Once some degree of rapport is established, this construction incorporates and utilizes otherwise resistant behaviours.
"The more you try to resist going into a trance, the more you find your eyes wanting to shut all by themselves."

10. **Tag Question:** A question added at the end of a statement/question, designed to soften resistance. It is used to ratify to the listener that he has or will actually manifest the action. It has the structure of a question and often the tonality of a statement.
"Your perception of life is changing, isn't it?!"
"We all read that last statement…….didn't we?!"

11. **Lack of Referential Index:** An expression without specific reference to any portion of the speaker's/listener's experience.
"People can change." "Things have always been this way."

12. **Comparative Deletion (Unspecified Comparison):** A comparison is made without specific reference to what or to whom it is being compared.
"You will enjoy it more." Or "That one is better." "I'm too fat."

13. **Pace Current Experience:** Using undeniable truths about what's in front of you and commenting on that to induce the relationship of the unconscious mind.

"You are sitting here, breathing into your body..." "As you sit or stand here, reading this book, you know it's going in on many levels and you will be able to use it......"

"As you are gathered here, in this meeting this morning, all of you are waiting with baited breath to what will be the outcome at the end of the day..."

14. **Double Bind:** Invites choice within a larger context of 'no choice'. Every avenue leads you to ONE outcome.

"Would you like the appointment on Tuesday or Wednesday?" "Do you want to begin now or in a few minutes?" Or "Do you want to go into trance before or after you sit down?" "Would you like the blue phone or the red one?" "Have you already decided to do the Master Practitioner course with us, or are you thinking of one more question to answer before you decide..."

15. **Embedded Commands:** This is a command that forms part of a larger sentence that is marked by using italics or a subtle change in voice tonality or body language and is picked up by the reader's or listener's unconscious.

"I will not suggest to you that *change is easy.*" Or "Do you think this is an intellectual debate about *the way your mind works is incredible....*" or "Perhaps you can *learn this material easily.*"

16. **Conversational Postulate:** Are questions that operate at multiple levels. Although they require only a simple yes or no answer, they invite you to engage in an activity in some way, yet with the authority taken out. Often they contain an embedded command.

"Can you open the door?" Or "Can you choose to change?"
Is it possible that you can make me some tea?"
"I'm wondering if you can go into a trance easily?"

17. **Extended Quote:** Is a rambling context for the delivery of information that may be in the format of a command. The listener's brain gets tired of the ramble and gives up...just in time for you to plant some important messages.

"Many years ago, I remember meeting a wise old man who taught me many useful things. I cherished all of his advice. I remember Dorren Boonzaier was on one of my courses and he reminded me of another seminar I had run many years before. One particular day he said to me...... "Change is easy and can be fun".

18. **Selectional Restriction Violation:** Attributing intelligence or animation to inanimate objects.

"Your chair can support you as you make these changes." Or "Your diary tells interesting tales." "The walls have ears." "Results tell us......"

19. **Ambiguity:** Lack of specificity

a. Phonological: "your" and "you're" —"hear, here", same sound, different meaning.

b. Syntactic: More than one possible meaning. "Shooting stars" "sex cells" "buy now..." or "leadership shows" - the syntax is uncertain within the context, i.e. adjectives, verbs or nouns?

c. Scope: "Speaking to you as a changed person ..." (Who is the changed person?) Or "The old men and women ..." - the context does not reveal the scope to which a verb or modifier applies.

d. Punctuation: is unexpected and does not 'follow the rules', i.e. Improper pauses, rambling sentences, incomplete sentences - all of which ultimately force the listener to 'mind read'. "Hand me your watch - how quickly you go into a trance."

20. **Utilization:** Takes advantage of everything in the listener's experience (both internal and external environments) to support the intention of the speaker.

Client says: "I don't understand." Response: "That's right...you don't understand, yet, because you've not asked the one question that will allow the information to fall easily and comfortably into place."

At the beginning of my career, I was seeing an important client and some road works started across the street. I immediately said, "Let that hammering be the hammering out of the old, past useless stuff in your life that isn't wanted anymore." We didn't hear the road works after that!

21. 'Away froms' or Negative Commands

Use the inability of your unconscious to comprehend language constructions that use complex negatives (No, Not, Don't, etc.). For instance, if someone were to say, "Don't think about a red tree in a blue field," what happens? Using negative language consciously can cause certain brain types to respond in the areas you want them to. 'Away froms', can be thought of as guiding the listener to the red tree, even though you've paced them 'not' to. Since the unconscious cannot process a complex negative, only the thing(s) you have mentioned remains in their system.

"Don't relax your mind too quickly as I want to be able to talk not only to your unconscious but your conscious mind too, before you let go and listen deeply. . . "

"It's important that you don't buy into this idea until you know you want it more than the old ones you've been using."

"Don't make any changes unless you really want to...and only you will know what changes you don't want as much as you know what you do...."

As you can see, the Milton Model comes to life in the context you are in. They are as easy to use in business as in therapy. In fact, now that you are aware of them, you'll start to hear them everywhere!

Business Example:

"You may be wondering what's on the agenda today", (mind read, yet it's causing the group to bond already as it's utilizing a wide view of the group nobody can disagree with), ..."and as you are all here listening to what is possible from being together for a short time.." (pacing current experience, of course they are all there listening, unless they fell asleep); "I'd like to expand on what you thought may be a limited experience and show you all the possibilities available today..". (pacing again any negativity, 'possibilities' is a nominalisation, plus it's a modal operator inside their own minds).

Then you'd go on to put some meat on the bones; yet, at the very least you have the vast amount of the group listening by now!

Chapter 11
The Meta Model

You will notice that many of these language patterns are identical to those of the Milton Model. The difference being that for the Meta Model, the client is being vague and we ask specific questions to assist them in getting clarity on their issue/problem. With the Milton Model we are being vague to deliberately bypass the conscious mind gate keepers!

Most people think that when they speak, they are describing the world at hand. It can't be further from the truth. Because our worlds are made from distorting, deleting and generalising, we are actually creating the world newly every time we utter a sound. Therefore, with this in mind, you can dissemble any un-empowering constructs in language with unique confidence that the client/learner can make a new fire to put logs on.

Distinguishing the Meta Model

Imagine there's a dark room. You're being paid one million pounds to find out exactly what's in that room and you've got five minutes to do it. The person you're questioning only gives you big picture answers and your job would be how to get that person, out of that big picture into specifics. They might say, "Oh yeah, it's a room." And you say, "OK, what's in the room?" "Oh, lots of things." "What's on the floor?"

You've got five minutes to find out exactly what's in every single corner, what's on the walls. What's inside the box over there, what's inside that? You want fact, fact, and fact, and you want to dig down into what's NOT being said. That's where the Meta Model would come in.

I remember one time a story about a guy who was on a self-development introductory evening course and they're selling possibilities. So there's nothing tangible to sell. There's nothing wrong with the course by the way, they're just selling life possibilities.

How do you sell a possibility? Well you have to be very abstract about it. So they say, "We promise you a breakthrough on this course."

There was this guy there, and I think he had the Meta Model kind of built into him. I think he was a built-in Meta Monster, as it were, and he just kept using (what we would call) the Meta Model patterns.

So they would say "Well, we promise you a breakthrough on this course."And he would say "What kind of breakthrough?" And they'd say "A breakthrough in the possibility of who you are!"And he would say "What you mean, 'the possibility'? And what do you mean by 'of who I am'?"

And this went on. Now they could only speak abstract language to sell this course and he just kept asking very specific questions. Then they got two organizers from the course to guide this guy out of the room because they couldn't handle it any more!

Abstract cannot handle specificity. Because you have to get more specific and you'll lose the ambience of a meeting if it gets too specific. Think of train spotters and hippies, not a great team!

And of course it goes deeper than that. People have hidden truths that they don't even know about themselves. The Meta Model goes about finding those too.

The Meta Model, according to the history that I know, was arrived at by the originators of NLP going out and modelling Virginia Satir. She was known as a family therapist. She would go into people's homes and people's families and she would simply ask questions.

Because of the intention, and obviously the consciousness of what she was doing with her languaging and the actual questions themselves, what people would discover is that they would come down inside the truth of a reality that they hadn't seen before.

The truth of the relationships had been buried so deep under the normal kind of language patterns that arrive in your head, that they were like treasure chests, waiting to be discovered again.

So, the theory is this; underneath the habitual languaging that you're normally doing in your head every day there is a truth and there are truths of your reality.

When you can dig down and find these truths, the problem, when exposed for the reality that it is, often just disappears or at the very least it loosens itself up.

The diagram we saw from The Human Communication Model illustrates that what your filter systems claim to be reality, are simply more 'maps of the territories' and not real at all. In other words what you perceive is, in fact, a projection derived from information passing through the filter systems.

More on Deletion, Distortion and Generalization (See also chapter 1 on The Human Communication Model).

As described by Bandler and Grinder, (see also chapter 1 The Human Communication Model) "Deletion is a process by which we selectively pay attention to certain dimensions of our experience and exclude others". Take, for example, the ability that people have to filter out or exclude all other sounds in a room full of people talking in order to listen to one particular person's voice.

For instance, a trainer friend of mine (I mention trainer to give you the fact that she has been specifically trained in cognitive skills, especially awareness), was waiting in Sweden for a train.

In Sweden trains almost always run on time, so she was there at the right time. After she noticed the train was late, she asked the stationmaster where it was. He replied that the train had come in... while she was sitting there, and then left! So she had deleted a whole train, noise and all!!

Which may make you ask the question, how much of life are we all deleting to suit our filtering systems of life?

Distortion is the process that allows us to make huge paradigm shifts in our experience of sensory data. Fantasy, for example, allows us to manipulate our internal worlds to suit what we either want to see/experience or what we expect to experience (perception is projection). Distortion can also prepare for experiences before they occur.

How this is useful when using language is to notice the generalizations in other's language to challenge them. Statements such as "He doesn't love me because he didn't buy me flowers on Tuesday", may be distorting any reality that may have been in place. Or "The stories I was told as a child were given to me to make me smaller and lose confidence". As much as that may be true to the person, the reality has been distorted to suit the storyteller.

Generalization is the process by which elements or pieces of a person's model become detached from their original experience and come to represent the entire category of which the experience is an example. Our ability to generalize is essential to coping with the world. The same process of generalization may lead a human being to establish a rule such as, "I don't express my feelings."

The function of the Meta Model is to help us identify lost language in their 'reality' of life as they are trying to express it, and to use the Meta Model to recover the lost linguistics.

Definition
The Meta Model is a method for helping someone get from the 'poor' internal word maps back to the specific sensory-based experiences they are based on. It is here in the information-rich specific experiences that useful changes can be made that will result in changes in behaviour.

What follows is a description of the different types of 'sloppy thinking' and examples of such. You will find a table at the end of the section that summarises the Meta Model.

The Meta Model language patterns (much of this was based on the work of family therapist Virginia Satir, gestalt therapist Fritz Perls and linguistic patterns from transformational syntax), yields a fuller representation of the client's model of the world.

The linguistic deep structure from which the persons' initial verbal expressions (or surface structure), were derived by offering challenges to its limits, the distortions, generalizations or deletions in the speaker's language. You will be digging down to specificity. And what's the specificity?

It's simply the specificity of the truth of the problem as they are holding it inside themselves. Now, here's the beauty - when they find the truth of the situation, it's often about them and not about anybody else. There'll be a responsible statement down deep inside them that they know they're causing this problem in some way or other.

When I say responsible or 'causing', I simply mean they will find a relationship between them and the issue that is causing them a problem. When you use the Meta Model gracefully, you'll find you dig down to where they're responsible and there'll be a language pattern down there which says it all. The fact is they just haven't uncovered that language pattern successfully just yet; all they're used to is the story of the problem whirring round and round and round in their own head.

You've probably noticed that yourself sometimes when you've had a problem. For example, you might have split up with your partner or there is a relationship in your business that's not going well or your money or something.

All that happens in your head is the same stories go round and round and round and you go and tell ten people and they all agree with you, or they don't agree with you but it doesn't change the story and it doesn't change the feeling inside. What this model does, it allows the gates of perception to open so you can begin to see in and peer into the reality of how you've held the problem inside.

I remember I was working at a school and there was a mother was having a problem with a pupil, so we had the mother into the office and she expressed a statement which might be kind of frightening to some people: "My son is hurting me" she said, and I said "Well how, specifically?" And then she said, "Well, he hits me!"

Some people might just stop there and say, oh, this is a big problem, there's violence here, you know and something's really happening, so, but knowing my Meta Model basically I'm going to ask another question which is, "OK, so, how hard and where?" And then she just says, "Oh, he doesn't know what he's doing."

What your job in hand here is to find the facts, whilst giving a bit of space to the 'story' being presented. Basically the mother's mind is going round and round and round because she's got a problem and she doesn't know what to do about it. Now, when I dug down deep enough I found that the hitting wasn't actually a big problem at all, it was how she didn't feel loved as a mother!

When people expose these truths often it's quite emotional and then the problem will disappear and they'll recognise that their own perception of the incident, being uncovered, allows it to disappear and disable itself.

When you recognise that a person has a way of speaking (and listening) that gets in the way of their success or happiness it is very tempting to want to tell them the error of their ways. After all, once you point out to them how ineffective they are being they will thank you and change their ways, right?

Obviously not! None of us like being told that we are wrong and that the speaker is right. So we energetically defend our beliefs, even the daft ones. In fact, the strength with which we adhere to our positions reflects the degree to which we have had to defend them!

The more you argue with a person and tell them how wrong they are the more you strengthen the language patterns that you wish to loosen. What to do?

Use the Meta Model. Add in huge amounts of rapport, good observational skills and the ability to be quiet while the other person thinks things through after you have asked a pertinent question. .

More examples of the Meta Model in action

Let's say, for example, that Jack says, "I can tell I won't do well in this subject by the looks the teacher gives me! That makes me sad because I never have any luck with teachers."
At first glance/hearing these are fairly understandable comments, yet when we apply the Meta Model to it we learn a little more...

A) Jack believes he can read the teacher's mind. This is an erroneous belief unless he is a very gifted clairvoyant!

B) He also believes that the appearance of her facial muscles enables him to predict what her likely response will be (check back on the mind reading errors from sensory awareness). In reality he is looking at her expression and deciding things from his own 'map of the territory' and not from sensory awareness purely.

C) He has a very limiting belief that he never has any 'luck with teachers'. This is a generalisation - a belief which rests on skimpy and carefully selected evidence. While it is possible that it is true this is rather unlikely. What is more likely is that he has is using the memory of a number of set-backs to generalise the past, to predict that the future will simply be more of the same - and to trap himself in a prison of his own debilitating beliefs.

D) In saying that 'this makes me sad,' Jack is announcing that he believes that his emotions are the result of outside events over which he has no control. But the way in which he announces this ensures that be remains a victim - since his comment implies no ownership of the difficulty! He 'is' a victim, but a victim of his own thinking rather than of events.

To assist Jack we could use the Meta Model to alert him to how his predicament is resulting from his own less-than-useful thinking. And, rather than lecture him on the error of his ways, we can do this in the most subtle manner - by simply asking a seemingly innocuous question or two.

We'll come on to these shortly. We have distinguished a finite amount of 'sloppy thinking' patterns and how to challenge them. There is a table further on in this chapter to assist you in learning these.

Firstly, you'll need some of these distinctions in your own mind. We'll start from distortions (remember that our sloppy thinking has derived from distortions, deletions and generalizations of the whole truth).

Presuppositions (under the bigger heading Distortions)

Presupposition refers to an assumption whereby the truth is taken for granted.

Crucially, negation of an expression does not change its presuppositions: I want to do it again and I don't want to do it again both mean that the subject has done it already one or more times:

My school is good and my school is not good both mean that the subject has a school to go to. In this respect, presupposition is distinguished from entailment and implication. For example, the president was assassinated entails that the president is dead, but if the expression is negated, the entailment is not necessarily true.

Example 1:
- "My teacher is terrible."
- Presupposition: You have a teacher and you think he/she is terrible in some way.

- Challenge: "How exactly is he/she terrible?" (Recovers lost information).

Example 2:
- "Do you want me to do it again?"
- Presupposition: I have done it already, at least once.
- Challenge: "Have you done it before, properly yet?"

Example 3:
- "My mum is as lazy as me, that's why I can't do it."
- Presuppositions: You have a mother; you say she's lazy.

Challenge: "Am I to assume that you are wanting the same bad habits?" (At least you will get more information about the motivation of the pupil).Have a go at drafting your own example:

Cause-Effect
Cause-effect, the inappropriate use of causal thinking (x means y, x makes me y, or x makes y happen) is considered semantically ill formed and unacceptable.

Causality always implies at least some relationship of dependency between the cause and the effect. For example, deeming something a cause may imply that, all other things being equal, if the cause occurs the effect does as well, or at least that the probability of the effect occurring increases.

Example 1:
- "That comment makes me angry."
- Challenge: "If it weren't for that comment, you would not be angry?"

Example 2:
- "Being late means I can't catch up."
   Challenge: "How, specifically, does you being late mean you are choosing not to catch up.?"

Mind Read
Mind-reading violation occurs when someone claims to think they know what another is thinking without verification.

Example:
- Jack says "I can tell I won't do well in this subject by the looks the teacher gives me! That makes me sad because I never have any luck with teachers."

   Challenge: "How do you know that look from the teacher means you won't do well?

- "You don't like me."
   Challenge: "Have I told you I don't like you?" "What informs you?"

Nominalization

Nominalization occurs when a verb is transformed/used as a noun. A dynamic process (i.e. a verb) is transformed into something static (i.e. a noun). It's like taking a snapshot of a moving object, you don't see the movement any more, just the (static) object.

What we are looking to do is retrieve lost information and look at the process the person is present to, rather than the "labels" that are apparent.

Example:
* "The communication in this company is poor."
   Challenge: "How could we communicate more effectively?"
   "Who is not communicating with whom?"

* "They need my decision by Monday."
   Challenge: "What are you deciding?" "What decision?"

Note: there are 2 simple tests that can be used to determine if a word or expression is a nominalization:

The wheelbarrow test: if you can put it into a wheelbarrow, it is NOT a nominalization. E.g. A house is a noun, but it is not a nominalization... as it is tangible, it can be put into a wheelbarrow (or a few wheelbarrows) and carried around. The phrase Quality Control fails the wheelbarrow test and is a nominalization.

Complex equivalence

Complex equivalence draws an unrelated conclusion from an event to create some supposed logic that, when scrutinised does not follow. Complex equivalence puts two things together, that may have no business being together, but can sound plausible.

Example:

1. "And now the secretary has left, I'll have twice as much work by the end of the year."
    Challenge: "Are you telling me your out-tray depended entirely on your secretary?"

2. "The results mean that I am not succeeding at all."
    Challenge: "Do you always judge yourself on results and not on what ongoing progress you can see from being here?"
    Another challenge: "You're not succeeding in the way you're looking at it". "How would you like to succeed in the future?"

Universals

Universals are words that want to encompass a great audience just via their utterance. Many people that try and use one-upmanship will use universals to gain authority for their cause.

Examples:
* "Every time I ask you a question, you grimace."
* "Everyone in the waiting room had at least one complaint against Dr. Parker."
* "There's always somebody in his class that will not pass."
* "All educated people are intelligent."

Universal quantifiers occur when someone attempts to characterize something as true for everything, everyone or all those in a set. This NLP Meta Model questions can be used when someone is generalizing too broadly.

Example:
* "My delegates are all lazy."
    Challenge: "All of them?" Or "Which delegates,

specifically?"

Modal operators

Modal operators are intuitively characterised by expressing a modal attitude, such as necessity (have to, must, should) or possibility (can, might, may) towards the proposition which it is applied to. (See also wishful thinking).

Example:
* "I can't pull myself together."
    Challenge: "What would happen if you did/didn't?"

Simple Deletions

In a simple deletion an important element in a statement is missing. For example: "Go and do it." "That is important." "I feel bad."

Key words to look out for are 'it' and 'that'.

The appropriate response would be to ask what, where or when exactly? "Go and do what exactly?"

Unspecified Verbs

In an unspecified verb it is not clear how the action creates or created the result.

Example:
    "I created a poor impression on them."
    Challenge: The appropriate response is to ask how
    exactly does taking "x" action lead to "y" result. "How
    exactly did you create a poor impression on whom
    exactly?" Or "What impression did you want?"

Comparative Deletion

Comparative Deletions are a comparative in which the starting point for comparison is not stated, which is also the deletion. These comparisons are frequently found in advertising. For example, in typical assertions such as "our chickens have more flavour", "our TV pictures are sharper" or "50% more", there is no mention of what it is they are comparing to. In some cases it is easy to infer what the missing element in a comparative is. In other cases the speaker or writer may have been deliberately vague in this regard, for example "Glasgow's miles better".

So, for example, if someone states that they are "too fat", they must be comparing without letting us know who (which is the deleted part). In China and some parts of Africa, it is/was good to be 'fatter' as it showed abundance and affluence!

Example:
* "I'm too fat."
  Challenge: "Compared to who?" (Gets you the lost information)

* "That wasn't the best plan."
  Challenge: "What were some of the other plans?"

* "I am a bad learner."
  Challenge: "Bad, compared to who?"

Lack of referential index

Lack of referential index, refers to the use of personal pronoun when the context is unknown, or cannot easily be understood based on the preceding sentences. For example, non-contextualised use of they, them, you.

Example

* "They say I should do my A-levels, but I don't know if I have the confidence."
   Challenge: "Who is it that says you should do your A-levels?" "What do you mean by confidence?"

* "Yeah, people have tried mind mapping before and it doesn't work for you."
   Challenge: "Wait; what people/who exactly?"

* "I hate watching England play. We always lose and it makes me depressed."
   Challenge: "By 'we', do you mean that you are part of the England team?"

* "Research has shown us that it's true".
   Challenge: "What research exactly?" "Who was it that made the research and what were they looking for?"

Lost Performative

Lost Performative makes reference to an action but the person who performed the action is unspecified.

Example:
   * "Her book wasn't highly acclaimed."
      Challenge:"Wasn't highly acclaimed by whom?" Or "How do you know that?"
   * "The lesson was judged as highly successful"
      Challenge: "Judged by whom?"

How to practice the Meta Model

1) Take one category at a time and practice it for a week or two.

2) Listen for the Meta Model violation (where the speakers' language deletes, distorts or generalises a portion of the whole story) and make mental notes to what language is missing. If you feel confident, interrupt the violations and ask for clarity (in as polite a way as is possible) - otherwise you are unlikely to take a very active role on the conversation!

3) The Meta Model 'challenges' or coaching questions need to be used with great caution. Use the challenges when you have very good rapport and calibration (ways to determine what you see in front of you specifically) skills.

4) Be careful to avoid overusing the coaching questions - otherwise the Meta Model can become an interrogation tool.

The Meta Model is a great tool in problem solving and troubleshooting. It's excellent for uncovering roots of people's problems when you're doing one to one with people and it's a very good business tool as well.

As a manager, or if you're on the upline somewhere in a networking group, then asking specific questions that dig down directly, vertically, into the truth of various problems assists greatly in the quality of expression of your group.

Chapter 12
Submodalities

Submodalities in NLP are fine distinctions or the subsets of the Modalities (VAKOG & Ai) and are part of each representational system that encode and give meaning to our experiences.

People have known about and worked with Submodalities for centuries. For example, Aristotle referred to qualities of the senses (which we refer to as the modalities), but apparently did not use the term sub-modalities.

They are the building blocks of the representational systems by which we code, order and give meaning to our lives. Submodalities are how we structure our experiences at the smallest level of conscious understanding.

How do you know what you like and what you don't like? You code the two different kinds of familiarity with different qualities of meaning. We create meaning by using different Submodalities to encode them and cause differences (you don't want to encode poison in the wrong place of course).

Changing Submodalities is a very effective and powerful way of changing the meaning of an experience. When we set a goal, for example, the more attention we pay to the Submodalities, the more we can feel it and therefore pre-experience it!

From Modalities to Sub-modalities

The five basic senses: visual, auditory, kinaesthetic, olfactory and gustatory (not forgettng the labelling system or Ai) are referred to as the representational system or modalities. For each of these modalities, we can have finer distinctions. We could describe a picture as being black and white or colour, or it could also be bright or dim. Sounds could be loud or soft, or coming from a particular direction. Feelings could be in different parts of the body or have different temperatures. Smells could be pleasant or offensive, strong or light. Taste could be sweet or bitter or strong or mild.

Research within NLP states that the brain often uses these structural elements as a way to 'know' how it feels about them, and what they signify internally. In effect we now have access to the very coding that links our specific internal 'library' to emotions and other associates about the outside world.

The great thing about Submodalities is that they are easy to use and very quick. As a practitioner you need very limited set up to use them and can release something as significant as a phobia in ten minutes or so!

Submodalities are key components to many of the NLP change techniques. Submodalities, by themselves or as part of other techniques, have been used to assist people to stop smoking, change eating habits, address compulsion issues, change beliefs and values, enhance motivation, move from stress to relaxation and address phobias. More or less anything to do with the human condition!

Distinctions in Submodalities

Each person's brain codes emotional significance differently through variations in mental "image" or representation. Examples found include people whose unconscious minds place black borders around bad memories, people for whom visual images seen dimly are less compelling than those seen brightly, people for whom a subjectively 'good' memory is accompanied by one kind of sound whilst a 'bad' memory is accompanied by another, and so on.

In visual terms, common visual distinctions include: location, brightness, degree of colour (saturation), size, distance, sharpness, focus, and so on. In auditory; loudness, pitch, tonal range, distance, clarity, timbre, and so on.

With feelings, it will be intensity, heat, cold, location of feeling, quality, etc.

Ordinarily, one can establish these by asking questions

"This image –are you looking through your own eyes or seeing your whole self in the picture (that's if they see a picture at all), Is it near or far? Where is the picture? (Get them to point at it), is it bright, or dim? Coloured or black and white? Is it big or small? In focus, or out of focus?"

"This sound - is it loud or soft? Is it high pitched or low pitched? Does it have a range? Is it near or far? Is it one point source or spread out? Where is it coming from? Is it clear or muffled?"

"That feeling in your body - where exactly is it? Does it have a size? A temperature? Does it stay the same, or does it move at all? Does it have a texture? Is it hard or soft?"

"This voice in your head; is it loud or soft. Who does it sound like?" When you have the internal representation of the 'thing' itself, you have the valuable code, which then can be changed or associated elsewhere.

Speed

Working quickly when with a client is essential in getting results. Because you are accessing the very code that the mind and body depend upon to give entry to locked out areas, you'll need to keep asking questions directed at the unconscious part of the clients mind. If you move too slowly, the mind can wonder a bit and you've lost the exact coding for your clients safety deposit box!

There will be a handful of such distinctions which are 'critical' to emotional perception, and thus to their mental processing. For example, these might be Submodalities that distinguish optimistic thoughts from depressive ones, or which distinguish compelling and important thoughts from less compelling ones.

For any given individual, a Submodality that turns out to be critical in how a memory or thought is subjectively experienced is known as a critical Submodality or *driver*.

Drivers in Submodalities

A driver is simply one of the critical submodalities that is making the difference to the whole scene. It's a piece of the jigsaw that makes the whole thing come to life, or not.

If you had a picture in your mind of dog poo; what's the one piece that makes it disgusting? Maybe we have to make it steaming? Perhaps the colour? Is it runny that makes it vile? Is it the location you see it in, the context?

Any one of these criteria will determine which of the submodalities is the critical one, called a driver.

These *drivers* differ between people, and can be identified by a process in NLP called contrastive analysis & mapping across Submodalities. A change within these critical Submodalities will often correlate with a near-immediate subjective change in the emotion or shift in the problem that was being presented.

If you start to distinguish your internal world of Submodalities as your library of codes, you start to have access to your inner game!

When we code a painful memory as associated, with a close-in image and loud sound, bright, three-dimensional, etc., we encode it with a structure that says, "Enter into that experience again and feel distressed, angry, fearful, upset, etc." That's the unconscious part.

Of course not every person will have the same code, but you can expect the mind to put bright, loud, intense and close things for the immediate attention of the experiencer!

Which brings us onto my favourite topic – reality. As we have already learned from The Human Communication Model, there is no IS reality; therefore each one of us makes these realities up and then puts wood on the fire every time we visit or revisit them.

Here the Submodalities encode the higher evaluative frame that essentially gives the behavioural Equivalent for: "Real, Close, Now, Associated." Yet that's not reality, it's just a message from the unconscious mind about perceived reality.

In this, the quality of Submodality distinctions works as the "switch" to experience.

It is experience, yet only the learned or programmed one. That's how and why we can make quick and possibly lasting changes using Submodalities. The mind and body know that the programmed realities are not absolutely real.

Distinguishing associated and dissociated

Associated/Dissociated is important in any intervention and especially submodalities where you are working with micro messages of a clients internal world.

Associated and dissociated refers to whether or not you are connected to the event intimately or not. In a visual representation, you are associated if you are inside your body, looking through your own eyes and don't see your whole self. If you can see yourself in the picture, then we say you are dissociated.

If you are associated in a memory, then your feelings (happy, sad, fearful) about that memory will probably be more intense. If you are dissociated, this is more like watching pictures (in a visual representation) or a movie of your life, rather than being there (on the playing field) and any feelings will be less intense or not present at all. When you come to perform an intervention, knowing which of these you'll use will be critical to how the client can either get into the issue or get out of the issue!

The Swish Pattern

The Swish Pattern is a useful technique to help people address an unwanted state or behaviour response to an event (or trigger) by changing key Submodalities of the event.

Compulsive or obsessive behaviours, such as an uncontrollable desire to bite your nails, smoke, eat certain foods, or habits are often linked with a trigger or cue image.

We are going to shift quickly from one image, (which contains drivers, or key Submodalities) to another predetermined set of key Submodalities.

Simply, we are instructing the unconscious mind: Not this — THIS!

Keys to Successful Swish Patterns

1. Have your client identify a specific behaviour that he wishes to change and the cue image (trigger) that starts the process.
2. Have your client identify a new self-image with the desired behaviour(s) that satisfies the positive intent of the undesired behaviour. Have them generate a picture of this new self-image.
Have the client assess the impact of this new behaviour on himself (what will he have to give up or take on), his family, friends, co-workers, community, etc.

Swish patterns are for the purpose of creating momentum toward a compelling future.

The Swish Pattern installs choices for a new way of life rather than to change or remove old habits.

1. Get the picture that represents the habit or situation you would like to change. (When you think of_____, do you have a picture?")
2. Get a picture of the type of person you would like to be. ("How would you like to be instead? When you think of that do you have a picture?")
3. Change the visual intensity of the desired state (brightness, size, distance, etc.) for the most "real" or most positive Kinaesthetic.
4. Bring back the old picture (#1), now step into the picture, fully

associated.

5. Now insert in the lower left hand corner, a small, dark picture of the desired state.

6. Simultaneously, have picture of current state rapidly shrink and recede to a distant point while dark picture explodes into full view. (This can be accompanied by either an internal or external SWIIISSH sound, but is not necessary—speed is!)

7. Repeat #6 a minimum of five times. Enjoy the results!

Notes To Keep In Mind

A.   Be fully associated in old pattern.

B.   Have detailed sensory-specific representations in the desired state.

C.   If client is associated in final picture = OUTCOME

D.   If client is disassociated in the final picture = DIRECTION (This is usually preferred to create a compelling future.)

E.   Make sure to have a break state between each Swish

Pattern so as not to loop them. Close eyes during each step of the process and open them between steps.

Submodalities Swish Pattern Script

1. Elicit Present State or Behaviour: "How do you know it's time to _____? (e.g. Feel bad.) When you think of that _____ (State or Behaviour) do you have a picture?" (Break State)

2. Elicit Desired State: "How would you like to (feel/act) instead? When you think of that _____ (State or Behaviour) do you have a picture?

3. If desired, assist client in adjusting the visual intensity of the Desired State for the most positive kinaesthetic.

4. "Good, now step out of the picture, so you see your body in the picture. (Break State)

5. "Good, now can you take the old picture and bring it up on the screen? Make sure that you are looking through your own eyes."

6. "As you have the old picture on the screen, can you see the new picture in the lower left hand corner, small and dark?
Make sure you see your body in the picture."

7. "Now have the picture explode big and bright, and have it explode up so that it covers the old picture, while the old picture shrinks down and becomes small and dark in the lower left hand corner, and do that as quickly as sssswishhhhh."

8. "Good, sssswishhhhh."

9. "Now, clear the screen."

10. Repeat steps 5, 6, 8, and 9 until the unwanted state or behaviour is not accessible.

Test and future pace. Test: Set the trigger off (if you can). Future pace: "Go into the future and notice how you react now."

Submodalities Like to Dislike Script

1. "Can you think of something that you like but wish you did not? Good, what is it? As you think about that, do you have a picture?" (Elicit the Submodalities.)

2. "Can you think of something which is similar, but which you absolutely dislike. For example, ice cream and yoghurt. (Elicit the Submodalities. The location should be different!)

3. Change the Submodalities of #1 into the Submodalities of #2.

Test: Now, what about that thing you used to like? How is it different?

Submodalities Belief Change Script

1. "Can you think of a limiting belief about yourself that you wish you did not have? Good, what is it? As you think about that belief, do you have a picture?" (Elicit the Submodalities.)

2. "Can you think of a belief which is no longer true. For example, perhaps you used to be a smoker. Someone who was a smoker, used to believe they were a smoker, but now they no longer believe that. Or someone who used to own a new 1985 car, believed that they were a new car owner, but now they no longer do. Do you have something like that which used to be true for you, but no longer is? Good, what is it? As you think about that belief, do you have a picture?" (Elicit the Submodalities.)

3. Change the Submodalities of #1 into #2.

Test: Now, what do you think about that old belief?

1. "Can you think of a belief which for you is absolutely true? Like, for example, the belief that the sun is going to come up tomorrow. Do you believe that? (Or, the belief that it's good to breathe.) Good, what is it? As you think about that belief, do you have a picture?" (Elicit the Submodalities.)

2. "Can you think of a belief that you want to have, which is the opposite of the belief in #1? Good, what is it? As you think about that belief, do you have a picture?"

3. Change the Submodalities of #5 into #4.

Test: Now, what do you believe? Why do you believe you have this new belief?

Examples of Triggers in NLP Contexts

Like to Dislike

"When you think of that, do you have a picture?"

Swish

"How do you know it's time to....?"

Anchoring

"How does it feel when you are in that place/state/experience?"
"Can you remember a time when you were totally _____?"

Strategy

"Can you remember a time when you were buying something by yourself? Can you remember a specific time? As you remember that time, what was the very first thing that happened...?" "Where are you? Walk me through this scene".

Chapter 13
Anchoring

Anchoring has been around in the form we know it through NLP since William Twitmire and Ivan Pavlov.

Bill Twitmire was known in the early 1900's for his experiments on the knee jerk reaction. Pavlov for his famous experiments with dogs. Pavlov got the dogs excited by bringing in food and ringing a bell (or tuning fork). He then repeated this several times, until eventually the dogs would hear a bell and start salivating with not a morsel in sight!

What we are saying 100 years later is that whenever a person is in a highly stimulated state and a stimulus is applied (or around), the two get hard wired in exactly the same way the dogs became associated with the food and the bell.

There are many ways to use anchoring: Stage anchoring has been associated with hypnosis for many years and we have learned a lot about how to use it with clients from this medium.

Personally, I now use conversational anchoring, as I find it more quick, graceful and applicable to business situations. We thank John Overdurf for his contribution to this arena. I will show you both the conversational anchoring and then the tactile version.

Accessing Positive States

Based on the information so far, we are ready now to discover how to put people into a good state. Actually, if you did the rapport exercise, you already know how to do this. The process of going into rapport with someone does indeed put them into a good state with you. In fact, if you're pacing and leading the person, just you going into a certain state will lead them along for the ride.

So the first step in putting people into state is to establish rapport. The second step is to put yourself into the state you want to establish in them.

The next step is to notice what ticks their boxes as you are talking to them. You already have the art of sensory awareness, so now you know how to notice changes in their state.

To get more deeply into their states you also know the Meta Model, so you can use that to "chunk down" on good states! Just ask easy questions like, "What's it like when you are doing what you love?", or "What do you love to do?" Just watch them go into state and then ask questions like, "What's that like?" (At this time you get into the state you want them to access.)" For example, "What do you love to do?" They answer "Fishing." You say "So what's it like when you are fishing?" They say "Great!" So you say "What kind if great, what do you really love about being there?" Just keep digging for the gold and use your awareness to detect changes.

When you see those changes, anchor it by using your own body and voice to feed it back. You know when you are being successful when they light up as you feed the words and body language back to them.

If you get really stuck you can ask it the old way we used to do by asking, "Can you remember a time when you were fishing, OK now get inside your body or if you were looking for a decisive time when they made a decision easily and quickly, "when were you were totally decisive?" Or, "can you recall a time when you purchased something that you were very happy with?"

What will happen is that people will literally go inside and do a search of their memory to discover that particular time. If you have them do enough of that (such as happy buying state), they will connect (or link) you to that state.

One more thing you can do in advance is to set the frame about what you're going to do. Here are some nice frames to put around the process of putting someone into state:

"As we sit here talking about your business, I'm beginning to wonder if it would be appropriate to ask you now - what do you love about your business...?"

"That reminds me, can you remember what it's like to be totally decisive....now!"

"You know, I was wondering, what's it like when you're making a business decision that's a big win for you, making you lots of money?"

And you know what? They'll love the time with you....and so will you!!

Conversational Anchoring Script

For conversational anchoring, remember, this is all you need:

- CONTEXT
- TRIGGER
- STATE
- BEHAVIOUR

Question to elicit the states (+ body language + eye patterns)

1st choice Question (see Accessing Positive States on the previous pages) "what's it like when you're ....?"

2nd "Look if you were feeling confident right now, how would you be sitting in this chair?" Look for gestures etc...maybe get them to stand up!

3rd "Can you remember a time when...?" (Can be dissociated if used this way)

Then: THE MOVE (for collapsing a negative anchor).

"That's the way you've been, how do you want to be different?"

Look for them to access VR to VC with eye patterns and analogue markings.

Steps for the collapse

- Present state, trigger etc.

- Outcome state "how do you want to be different?"

- Then fish for pumped up outcome words feelings

- Attach resources to present state

- Condition the response (context, trigger, resource a few times in the same context they give you)

- Test: take them to trigger and let it run itself

- Future pace: go into future........(no deliberate anchoring)

So, when you have access to a state, the next step is to anchor it. And remember that a spontaneous state is usually more powerful than one that is induced. Whenever you find a state that you can use (whether it's in you or someone else), you can anchor it.

The first step is to put the person in state. You can use a spontaneous state, (asking the question "what's it like when..." will be a present tense state) or an induced state ("Can you remember a time...") It's important that the state be fully associated. Which means that the person is in their body, being there as opposed to thinking they are there. It's also important that the state be intense and congruent.

People go into states at different rates, so it's important that you calibrate the state, or you can ask them to tell you when they are fully into the state, at the peak of the experience. You can have them nod, move their head, or finger, or foot or whatever. Remember, in rapport, you feel what they feel, so if you trust yourself enough, you already know!

Application of a Conversational or Tactile Anchor

The second step, when they're at the peak is to watch what they do with their bodies, eyes, breathing, hands etc. Also take note of the words they use and how they say them. This will be the unique stimulus to fire it off again.

Notice that as the state begins to peak, the person should outwardly be showing you how they represent that internal state. It's almost as if they can't hold it inside anymore and it has to come out to be seen. It's at these points you'd consider the state to be at its peak and note all the behaviour because that's what you'll use later to fire it off again.

When you have access to that state, anchor it. You can anchor by using their body language, voice tonality and words. When they outwardly (and for them, extrovertly) show you the internal world on the outside, do it back to them and see if their mind and body agrees (calibrate them) with the way you do it back. If it works they will like it when you repeat the body language with the words and tone!

What you may want to do, in order to get a very intense (positive) state when you're working with someone, is to literally 'stack' anchors.

So you can use different occasions, contexts, events to get into several states and then you have a series of positive powerful states to use.

So you could use a context of love, confidence, power etc. and for each one say "What's it like to be in that place?""And what's that like?" "What is it exactly that you love about that?" Anything that chunks then down and gets them really associated. Now, you have captured these states and can bring them back just by repeating the body language and words/tones the same way.

If that isn't working, ask these questions..........

a. "Can you recall a time when you were totally capable?"
b. "Can you recall a time when you were totally loved?"
c. "Can you recall a time when you were totally powerful?"
d. "Can you recall a time when you laughed hysterically?"

Tactile (touching) anchoring

If you are doing tactile or kinaesthetic anchors, then they should start slightly before, and end right at the peak of the intense state or slightly before. An anchor should be applied for from five to fifteen seconds, so using a physiological (kinaesthetic) anchor you would hold the touch up to fifteen seconds.

You can also anchor all the states by touching the person in the same place in exactly the same way. Knuckles work well as the touch you give is easily replicable.

Break state

The next step is to change the person's state. Have them get out of the state they were in. Perhaps talk about something else. At least have them take a deep breath.

With conversational anchoring, set off the anchor by using the tone of voice, body language etc. Or if you are using tactile anchors, apply it (the anchor) in exactly the same way on a knuckle or replicable place on their body, and discover if they go back into state. Knuckles are the best place to touch, as they are unique and the touch replicable.

There are five keys to successful anchoring: ITURN can be easy to remember.

1.   The first is the **Intensity** of the response, or the congruity of the state. In anchoring, we're looking for a fully associated intense state. You may ask, "Are you seeing yourself or are you in your own body?" We want them to be in their own body (associated).

2.   The second element is the **Timing** of the anchor. The anchor should be applied just before the peak. If you hold it too long, then you may find that the person has gone beyond the first experience into a second, into another state, and the two states may be linked.

3.   In tactile anchoring, the stimulus should also be **Unique (in conversational anchoring the stimulus is always unique by default).** The uniqueness of the stimulus is important because if you set up an anchor on an area of the body (assuming a kinaesthetic anchor) that is touched a lot, such as a handshake, then the anchor will become weakened with time (diluted) because it will be set off by other people. So you will want to provide an anchor that is in a unique area of the body. Often an NLP professional will use an ear to set up an anchor or ask you to put a series of positive anchors in a fist.

(If you are using tactile anchors the next piece applies, if not then conversational anchors will be as good as you keep using the persons own version of the state.)

How long an anchor lasts depends specifically upon how unique the location is. If it's not an intense state that you're anchoring, or if you haven't stacked it, then the anchor will wear off or dilute itself more quickly. If the location is not unique it can be fired off so many times that it won't work again, because it won't be linked to the specific state.

4.   The next key is the **Replication** of the stimulus. The way that you apply (if conversational anchoring, it's how close you get to the persons unique way of representing their inner state), the anchor in setting it and in firing it off to test, need to be exactly the same every time. So if you're snapping your fingers or giving them a certain look, you need to do it the same way every time. That anchor needs to be fed back to the person in exactly the same way it was set.

5.   **Number** of times: How many anchors you have discovered and are able to fire off. If it were tactile anchoring, it would be the number of anchors you have established on a knuckle, for instance.

Collapsing Anchors

All human change (All? Yes, all) is nothing more than an integration of resources or a collapsing of realities, one into the other. The particular process of collapsing anchors involves taking a negative state, and integrating or collapsing it into a positive state. Doing this gives the person we're dealing with more neurological choice. One of the major premises of NLP is to increase the choices a person has.

So, if we find, for example, that every time a certain salesperson goes out to make a sale that they become negative. It may be because they're recalling all the times they've failed. If the two are linked, we can collapse the association of sales and failure, with a winning attitude, and give the salesperson the choice of feeling good about selling, too.

The process of collapsing anchors will free the salesperson from the necessity of having to access the negative state every time they go out and make a sales call.

The process of collapsing anchors is one of the more powerful processes in NLP, and this technique can also be used for collapsing anchors by yourself and it's also easy to use. I am going to show you ONE version of conversational anchoring and ONE version of tactile or kinaesthetic anchoring. Remember there are different ways of doing this!

1.   Ask the person to recall a series of positive experiences, and anchor each one. Stack the anchors. For example, when they couldn't lose, when they felt powerful, when they knew they could have it all, when they knew they could have whatever they wanted.

2.   If you are using conversational anchoring, you'll have to remember what they said or did when in an intense state. The easiest way is to feed it back and then you learn it easily. If you are using tactile anchors, then have them put all the experiences, one at a time, into their right hand, while you are firing off the original anchor that you have set, with each experience.

3.   In conversational anchoring, have them get into a powerful state, whilst talking about the problem state. Mix up both states, so the powerful states start to be introduced to the nervous system at the same time as the negative state is being recalled. The powerful one should end up winning (if it doesn't the powerful states were not properly set up or not powerful enough).

4.   If tactile, have them look at the right hand, and describe what those experiences look like. What do they say, or what do they sound like? What do they feel like? What is the shape, colour, size, sound, and smell. Make a fist, now, and hold on to all those positive experiences.

5.   In the tactile version, now have them put the negative experience into the left hand. (If the negative experience is particularly strong, you can have the person put the negative experience into the left hand quickly without looking at it. If it's

not very strong, have them describe it as they did with the positive.)

You don't have to set an anchor for the negative experience other than the hand.

6.   Go back to the right hand. Have them notice those experiences again. Ask them again about some of the Submodalities, the smell, the sound, the colour, the brightness, and shape.

7.   Now, holding the right hand over the left hand, have them pour the positive experiences from the right hand, including the feelings and the sounds, into the left hand. Have them make a "sshhhh" (or any) noise as they do it. And have them continue pouring until the contents of both hands are the same. When both hands look, sound, and feel the same, then they can stop.

8.   Next, have them clap their hands together once, and then rub them together vigorously.

9.   Finally, have them look again and make sure that both hands are the same. If not, go back to #1.

10.   The negative experience in the left hand and the positive experience in the right hand will be linked in the neurology, so that the person will have more choice. The person can feel negative about the negative experience or they can feel positive about them. The negative will not have the hold over them that it had before. It's a very powerful process, by the way, and one that you can use on yourself or others to reduce the effect of negative experiences and to create new neurological choices.

11.   One important caution in this process is that the NLP Practitioner should be sure that the positive anchors are stronger than the negative anchors. What you're doing is diluting the negativity with the positively, neurologically. So it's a neurological dilution of the negative experience. However, if the negative experience is stronger than the positive, then the positive experiences will be diluted into the negative, which is not what you want. Typically,

an NLP professional will set a number of positive anchors before beginning this process, so that the negative experiences will be weaker than the positive ones. In addition, make sure that the person you're working with is dissociated from the negative experiences. Don't allow them to access the negative states too long, and make sure to get them out of the negative states.

12.　　Whether you have been using your voice and body alone or touching them with tactile techniques, the theory is still the same!

Outcome

The desired outcome for this section is for all participants to be able to anchor a specific state in a person, at any time in any modality.

Theory

A.　　Definition: Any time a person is in an associated, intense state, if at the peak of that experience, a specific stimulus is applied, then the two will be linked neurologically.

B.　　Anchoring can assist you in gaining access to past states and linking the past state to the present and the future.

Process:

The Four Steps to Anchoring:

1.　　Have the person recall a past vivid experience.
2.　　Provide a specific stimulus at the peak (see chart below)
3.　　Change the person's state
4.　　Set off the anchor to test

The Five Keys to Anchoring:

1.   Intensity of the Experience   I
2.   Timing of the Anchor   T
3.   Uniqueness of the Anchor   U
4.   Replication of the Stimulus   R
5.   Number of times   N

State Script for Tactile Anchoring

The best states to anchor are naturally occurring states. Next best are past, vivid, highly associated states. Least preferable are constructed states.

Question to elicit the states (+ body language + eye patterns):

1st choice Question "what's it like when you're ....?" "How specifically?" (Or any meta model questions).

2nd "Look, if you were feeling confident right now, how would you be sitting in this chair?" Look for gestures etc...maybe get them to stand up!

3rd "Can you remember a time when...?" "Can you remember a specific time? As you go back to that time now ... go right back to that time, float down into your body and see what you saw, hear what you heard, and really feel the feelings of being totally _____X'd_____". (Can be dissociated if use this way)

States for Stacking Anchors

To stack anchors, elicit several instances of states and anchor them via recognising the body language, tone of voice and words, then feed them back to test:

In tactile anchoring they would be touched in the same place. The state chosen for a particular stacked anchor can be the same or different.

Let your client come up with their own states: For instance, when you ask them "what's it like, fishing?" You want them to let you know what the state is.....

If you don't get anything from that (rarely if you are on the ball that day), you can give them clues to states such as these below:

• A time when you felt totally powerful.

• A time when you felt totally loved.

• A time when you really felt you could have whatever you wanted,

• A time when you felt you couldn't fail, when you could have it all.
• A time when you felt really energetic, when you had a ton of energy.
• A time when you fell down laughing.

• A time when you felt totally confident.

Chaining Anchors

Chaining is a technique that is used when the desired/resource state is significantly different from the present state.

1. Get in rapport.

2. Tell the client what you are about to do: "In just a moment I am going to do a process called 'Chaining Anchors' (explain), and that will necessitate that I touch you. Is that OK?"

3. Identify the undesirable present state (e.g. Procrastination), and decide on the positive/resource end state (e.g. Motivation).

4. Design the chain: Decide on what intermediate states are needed to lead to the end state.

Present State	Intermediate State #1	Intermediate State #2	End State

5. Elicit and anchor each state separately, beginning with the present state through the end state. (You may have to stack all states to get a high intensity.) Make sure that the subject is out of previous state prior to anchoring the next one. (Break State between states, especially between the last one and the first one.)

6. Test each state. Make sure that the client goes into each one.

7. Chain each state together firing #1 and when #1 is at its peak add #2, and then release #1. When #2 comes to the peak, add #3, then release #2. Add #4, etc. in the same way. (This is NOT a collapse because the two states do not peak at the same time.)

8. Test: Fire present state anchor. Client should end up in final state.

9. Ask the client, "Now how do you feel about _____." e.g. "How do you feel about procrastination?"

10. Future Pace: "Can you think of a time in the future which if it had happened in the past you would have _____ (e.g. Procrastinated) and tell me what happens instead?"

Chapter 14
Eye Patterns

Eye patterns were something that were being noticed by the originators of NLP at a very early stage of its evolution. In their work they began to notice that there appeared to be a correlation between where people's eyes look, to the kind of sensory language they are using. More particularly, they suggested the eyes move around when people are thinking and internally processing (prior to speaking), and that you can often see a correlation between what they then say and where their eyes were before they spoke.

Next time you're having a conversation with someone, pay particular attention to what happens to their eyes when they are thinking, particularly after you asked the question. Do you see any patterns or themes?

The originators of NLP sent out a 'scout' to discover more. From this work of Robert Dilts, they discovered that as people recall certain parts of information, their eyes will move to certain quadrants of their brain to access either visual, auditory, kinaesthetic or self talk. This then gives you a good idea about what that person is doing inside their mind as they try and recall information.

They observed patterns of relationship between the sensory-based language people use in general conversation, and their eye movements (known as eye accessing cues).

NLP also suggests that sometimes, such processing is associated with sensory word use; so a person asked what they liked about the beach, may flick their eyes briefly in some characteristic direction (visual memory access, often upwards), and then also use words that describe it in a visual sense e.g. "The sea looked lovely", and so on.

Likewise asked about a problem, someone may look in a different direction for a while (kinaesthetic access, typically downwards to their right) and then look puzzled and say "I just can't seem to get a grip on things".

Taken together, NLP suggests such eye accessing cues are idiosyncratic and habitual for each person, and may form significant clues as to how a person is processing or representing a problem to themselves unconsciously.

When you begin this journey into watching eye patterns, it's good to note that they will be either 'normally' organised or completely reversed.

We have not seen any deviants to the chart we show you on the next page. You always need to calibrate (look at the fact of the body and eyes) on the individual level, but once you have learnt someone's pattern of operating you can start to make predictions.

The common western layout of eye accessing cues is as follows

The Senses Are Also in Our Eyes

Auditory Cues

Remembering Sounds (Side Left)   **Constructing Sounds** (Side Right)

Kinaesthetic Eye Cues

Hearing Internal Dialogues/Chatter (Down Left)   **Accessing Touch, Taste, Smell, Feelings** (Down Right)

Visual Eye Cues

Remembering Pictures (Up Left)   **Making Pictures** (Defocussed)   **Constructing Pictures** (Up Right)

Normally Organized Person
As you Look at them

NLPworld

Visual Construct (VC) Top left quadrant
Visual Remembered (VR) Top right quadrant

Audio Construct (AC) Middle left quadrant
Audio Remembered (AR) Middle right quadrant

Tactile (K) Bottom left quadrant
Audio Internal (or AD) Bottom right quadrant

Questions to ask someone to find out what's happening........Watch the eye patterns!

1. Visual Remembered: Think of the colour of your car. What kind of pattern is on your bedspread? Think of the last time you saw someone running. Who were the first five people you saw this morning?

2. Visual Construction: Imagine an outline of yourself as you might look from six feet above us and see it turning into a city skyline. Can you imagine the top half of a toy dog on the bottom half of a green hippopotamus?

3. Auditory Remembered: Can you think of one of your favourite songs? Think of the sound of clapping. How does your car's engine sound?

4. Auditory Constructed: Imagine the sound of a train's whistle changing into the sound of pages turning. Can you now hear the sound of a saxophone and the sound of your mother's voice at the same time?

5. Auditory Digital (Internal Self Talk): Take a moment and listen to the sound of your own inner voice. How do you know it is your voice? In what types of situations do you talk to yourself the most? Think of the kinds of things that you say to yourself most often.

6. Kinaesthetic Remembered: (Tactile) When was the last time you felt really wet? Imagine the feelings of snow in your hands. What does a pine cone feel like? When was the last time you touched a hot cooking utensil? (Visceral/Emotional) Can you think of a time you felt satisfied about something you completed? Experience what it feels like to be exhausted. When was the last time you felt impatient?

7. Kinaesthetic Construction: (Tactile) Imagine the feelings of stickiness turning into the feelings of sand shifting between your fingers. Imagine the feelings of dog's fur turning into the feelings of soft butter. (Visceral/Emotional) Imagine the feelings of frustration turning into the feeling of being really motivated to do something. Imagine the feeling of being bored turning into feeling silly about feeling bored.

Application in the learning environment

In terms of learning and education, this can be really useful as you can begin to tell where your pupils (via their pupils), are trying to access information from and what strategies they are using to get their information.

For instance, if you ask a person to spell a word, and they are looking down to the ground to their right-hand side they will be accessing feelings, so it will be no wonder that John would not be a very good speller.

If you try to spell a word by feeling it, this is probably the worst strategy you could imagine. Also, if the person looks to their left hand side the middle (see diagram), they'll be trying to spell the word by hearing it phonologically: That's also not the best strategy to use! You can't even spell phonologically, phonologically!! Let's try....fonologically...nope!

You can improve people's spelling ability or learning ability by teaching them how to use the visual aspect of their brain. You'll see the remarkable effect it will have when you have learnt how to do this sufficiently.

Of course this isn't just useful for pupils, this will also be useful to you and any conversation negotiations situations where it's important you to know how the other person is processing their world.

Changing a poor spelling strategy

Pick somebody who spells particularly poorly and is motivated to spell differently and better. Ask them for a word that they cannot possibly spell.

Case study

Catherine Sprackling, at the time head of French at a Brighton school, performed this technique shortly after being trained how to use it.

What Catherine did was to take a pupil and choose a word he could not possibly spell and believed could never spell. Then she wrote that word on a piece of paper and chunked it into three parts, of relatively similar sizes.

She used her knowledge of anchoring to make the boy feel good about the prospect of learning (you could just ask the pupil if there's been a time when they didn't think they could learn something and then they did).

Catherine then showed the word, piece by piece (you can also make the chunks different colours to aid the visual aspects). She got him to recite each chunk of the word, whilst holding the word in his visual recall quadrant (VR), whilst he kept his head facing forwards. She would take the paper away each time but ask him to keep visualizing the chunk of word in his mind (watching his eye patterns to make sure they stay in visual recall).

Then finally, she took away all of the chunks and asked him to spell the whole word, which he did successfully first time. Then to the amazement of the rest of the classroom, she got him to spell the word backwards with no more revision. He did it perfectly!

Other uses of eye patterns

The best known therapeutic application of eye patterns has been undertaken by a woman called Francine Shapiro (1995) and is called EMDR which stands for eye movement desensitization and reprocessing. Her methods are now widely used in the process of therapy and although not fully understood they seem to work by linking the different areas of the brain together.

History of EMDR

Dr. Francine Shapiro, the creator of EMDR is a licensed psychologist and a senior research fellow at the Mental Research Institute in Palo Alto. She is the Executive Director of the EMDR Institute, which trains clinicians in the EMDR method. She is the recipient of the 1994 Distinguished Scientific Achievement Award presented by the California Psychological Association.

So, how does this work?
Like a narrative, a piece of writing, a script is an instrument for the management and effective control of a play, film or broadcast. In this counselling /therapeutic context scripts are the tools with which we manage our adult life. You could call them language patterns (and in this case they can be pictures, sounds, feelings carried in language).

From our earliest and formative years we build a library of scripts through and with which we respond and react to life. As with the section on anchoring, any stimulus is categorised and linked to our response and via our memory is stored in our database or library. What seems to happen is that certain areas of the brain or mind get under- used or not even accessed for varying reasons.

For example, we will have a family of scenes about school, which would include positive and negative affects depending on our relative success or failure to different aspects of our school experience.

These scenes will be held in VR, VC, AR, AC, K and AD. If a scene is too painful, that area will be avoided.

A friend of mine was asked a question by a teacher once and he looked up and to his left (visual recall or VR), the teacher then shouted, "It's not up there boy!" That area may well be painful to visit the next time he's looking for information!

With the exercise we are giving you here, you get a chance to link up all the different areas of the brain and literally exercise the different quadrants, linking them together so they all can work as efficiently as they can. By using a grid reference from each quadrant to every quadrant (map out the head and make a grid reference for every possible point of the eye patterns to each other)on the eye map and moving a finger line all the way around) accessing all the different areas. Take a look on YouTube for the BBC2 documentary for a visual image of EMDR in action.

Try this

1) Hold a pen out in front of you (about two feet in front your or another's face).

2) Move it to the periphery (boundary) of the eyes to the left, so without moving the head, the eyes can just about still see the tip of the pen.

3) Move the pen and whilst superimposing the virtual grid reference to your own face (or to another's face in front of you), follow the grid lines with the pen whilst keeping your head still and only moving your eyes.

4) Remember to go to the edge of the eyes' movements as you come

to each end of a line.

5) Follow every possible line and join all the lines up by following the tip of the pen with the eyes.

6) If you find any glitches (places where the eyes flicker or do not move along smoothly), you can move the pen up and down that line until the glitch rubs itself out.

At the very least, this exercise will increase the co-ordination of each quadrant of the brain, causing more communication between areas that may have been less flexible before. What this exercise does is to stretch the peripheries of vision, whilst connecting up every possible quadrant of the brain. This can help even the brightest of pupils, yet EMDR has had an amazing effect on all age ranges and in all sorts of different contexts.

Fourteen controlled studies support the efficacy of EMDR, making it the most thoroughly researched therapy method ever used in the treatment of trauma. The 5 most recent studies with individuals suffering from events such as rape, combat, loss of a loved one, accidents, natural disasters, etc. have found that 84-90% no longer had post-traumatic stress disorder after only three treatment sessions. A recent study financed by Kaiser Permanente revealed that EMDR was twice as effective in half the amount of time compared to the standard traditional care.

The major significance of EMDR is that it allows the brain to heal its psychological problems at the same rate as the rest of the body is healing its physical ailments. Because EMDR allows minds and body to heal at the same rate, it is effectively making time irrelevant in therapy. Given its wide application, EMDR promises to be one of the successful therapies of the future.

Chapter 15
NLP & Strategies

NLP was created somewhat as a result of Modelling. Bandler and Grinder's system for Modelling was essentially to discover somebody's belief systems, physiology, and mental strategies. In the process of modelling, they would elicit a person's internal program, which they called "mental syntax" or "strategy."

NLP focuses on strengthening your own internal resources so you can effect changes in your life. The solutions come directly from your subconscious mind, therefore is from the root of you; this ensures you are fully committed to making that change.

In Neuro-linguistic programming, a strategy is an internal and external sequence used to achieve a specific result. Strategies could be described as a sequence of representational systems and submodalities combined.

'Personal Strategies' has been formed to offer a comfortable and sympathetic solution for anyone wishing to make a change. Whether you are looking to change a habit or improve some areas of your life or improve existing strategies.

The formal definition through NLP of strategies

A specific syntax of external and internal experience which consistently produces an outcome. Human experience is an endless series of representations. To deal with this endless sequence it is useful to suspend the process, and contextualize it in terms of outcomes.

Types of strategies

Deep Love
Attraction
Buying
Selling
Eating
All Decisions
Health
Money

And.....just about anything you can think of that has internal and internal components!

Below, I give you the technical definition how it has traditionally be trained. However!! They are better learned by understanding the concept that all human experience has a structure to it, or strategy.

If you consider from an early age, we all got bits of information from modelling our parents and peers, you'll notice that we are like mini-movies with frame by frame construction of the things we do. Of course, life is moving fast, so we don't see the frames (just as in a movie you don't see the thousands of frames that make them up).

The way we can make use of these 'frames' in NLP is to be aware of the piece by piece process by which the client is making their strategies function. You have become aware of the eye patterns, so can notice what they are doing internally; the next step is piecing those eye patterns together with whatever the person is telling you about a situation.

Some of their strategy will be conscious, so that's what comes out of their mouth. Some of it will be unconscious, which is why you have to have the ability to read eye patterns.

The strategies will most likely have three or four steps maximum, so be aware to watch out for 'looping' where they are telling you again and again the same strategy.

QUESTIONS TO ELICIT STRATEGIES

Formal Strategy Elicitation - Script

Can you remember a time when you were completely X'd?
Can you remember a specific time? (For eliciting state strategies) OR Think back on when you made that decision.
(For eliciting action strategies)
And as you go back to that time now...
What was the very first thing that caused you to [be totally X'd / make that decision]?
* Was it something you saw (or the way someone looked at you)?
* Was it something you heard (or the tone of someone's voice)?
* Was it the touch of someone or something?
After that, what was the very next thing that happened [as you were totally X'd / that caused you to make that decision]?
* Did you picture something in your mind?

* Did you say something to yourself?
* Or did you have a certain feeling or emotion?
After that, did you know [you were totally X'd / it was time
to decide]? (If not, keep looping on question #4 and #5
until you have the complete strategy)

Deep Love Strategy Elicitation

Note: This should never be elicited while the client is looking at
you, the Practitioner, as it will fire off the strategy, which could
then be anchored to you.

1. How do you know someone else loves you?
2. Can you remember a time when you were totally loved?
   A specific time?

Here are some other questions that should trigger off a clients mind
into showing you their strategies: If these questions are what you
want to ask to get a response, ask them and watch the eye patterns
at the same tie listening to the predicates (VAKOG words).

What let you know it was time to decide?
When did you begin deciding?
How did you know it was time to decide?
Operate: How did you know there were alternatives?
How do you generate alternatives?
Test: How do you evaluate alternatives?
What has to be satisfied in order for you to decide?
Exit: How do you select which alternative to take?
How do you know (or what lets you know) that you have decided?
How using Strategy interventions can help:

Society can condition us all to follow and creates directions we have to travel, rather than allowing us real freedom to choose.

INSTALLING OR CHANGING STRATEGIES

* Rehearsing
* Reframing
* Metaphor
* Anchoring
* Dissociated state rehearsal

DESIGN PRINCIPLES

DESIGN
* Maintain the function.
* Intervene before the strategy goes haywire.
* Calibrate.
* Reframe or use Submodalities on unpleasant feelings or voices.
* Delete unnecessary steps.
* Make sure that the criteria are accessed sequentially and not simultaneously.
* Make least amount of change to get the results you want.

REDESIGN
* Make up what you think could work.
* Check your own strategy for applicability.
* Model someone else who has a good strategy.

"We are what we repeatedly do." Aristotle

So simply, to design and install a new strategy, you get them to make each frame (as if in a movie) and make it either VAKOG, to suit the successful completion of a new strategy.

For instance, if the client has a buying strategy that goes V - K. It's going to be VERY expensive to someone's pocket! To see something then feel like buying it without any criteria has emergency written all over it.

To redesign this one, you'd need to rehearse some AD (self talk or criteria) as one of the steps. You could slot some criteria (for instance "do I need this?" Or "is this on our shopping list?"), as step number two.

So now when they go shopping, they see something nice (V), have some thoughts about it (new design AD), then either satisfied that it's on the shopping list, feels good and buys it (K), or does not 'exit' to buy and carries on.

Chapter 16
Reframing

One of my favourite topics and experiences on trainings is teaching the art of reframing.

Obviously, reframing occurs in life regardless of NLP and is a common means by which meanings get created and lost in various situations, either deliberately or by happenstance.

The basis of reframing comes from the fact that the content or meaning of a situation is determined by the context it appears in, or what you choose to focus on.

For instance, I live in Brighton and when I look out of the training room window, I see the beach (yes lucky me). On that beach there also will be (according to the weather), people with not many clothes on.

And that's perfectly normal. But if one of those people, who are fine by us 200 metres away, came into our room, the whole room would be in disarray. Yet when we go to the beach for our tea, no-one will bat an eyelid!! So what's the difference. Context is all.

Reframing provides a new context or focus for your thoughts and actions. Just as a picture frame puts borders or boundaries on what you can see in a picture, the frames of reference can limit what you see as possible.

You and I are continually setting time frames, boundaries, limits, etc. on what you can and can't do - often without any real thought about the consequences or if the limitations are true.

Changing the frame of an experience can have a major influence on how you perceive, interpret and react to that experience. Being told that you have one hour to complete a task will most likely result in a different emotional state, approach and quality of work than if you are told that you have one week to accomplish the same task. This illustrates how a change in frame can have a significant impact on the way you feel about life.

The purpose of reframing is to unlock linguistic prisons that people have bound themselves into. There is a hieroglyph from Egypt, which shows a man with his hands bound. The Western translation of that is that the Egyptians had slaves: From my sources, I've been enlightened that the Egyptians did not have slaves but were a very abstract race. Therefore the symbol of a man who is bound, is bound by his habits only.

People have incarcerated themselves with guilt, doubt, judgment and they hold their own keys to the linguistic prison cells they gave themselves a life sentence on.

Our job as NLP practitioners is to free them from these sentences and cause at least a loosening of the prison walls.

Words (our wor'l'ds), are powerful entities so that reframes, when uttered with a an intention and enough consciousness, can free any person.

A classic example of a reframe by Milton Erickson concerns a father who complains at the stubbornness of his daughter. This results in a double reframe, in which Erickson points out two things to the father:

1. There are situations where she will need stubbornness, to protect herself or achieve something. In fact, Erickson points out, this will make her as successful as her father! Reframing switches to a context that makes the stubbornness relevant.

2. It is from the father himself that she has learned to be stubborn. By forcing the father to equate his own stubbornness with hers, this creates a context in which he either has to recognize the value of her stubbornness, or deny the value of his own.

One of the common challenges of family therapy is to help the parents let their children go. Independence is of course a negative goal. The parents have to gradually stop supporting their children, and the children have to gradually stop relying on their parents.

Virginia Satir often used the approach of creating an alternative goal for the parents by preparing themselves to be grandparents. In a typical case, a young woman consulted her; her parents had used their life savings to build an extension to their house where she was to live when she got married. (At this time, she was away at college, and had no steady boyfriend.)

Satir met the parents, and congratulated them for their willingness to participate so actively in the rearing of their (one-day-to-come) grandchildren, having babies crying through the night, toddlers crawling through the living rooms, toys strewn across the house and baby sitting.

She thus created a powerful positive image of the joys of grandparenthood; yet for some reason, the couple decided to rent the extra rooms out to mature lodgers instead, and save the money to support their grandchildren's education. When the daughter subsequently got married, she lived in a city some distance away with husband and baby, and the grandparents visited frequently, but not too frequently.

Why does this example count as reframing, rather than replacement? The alternative goal created by Satir was not an alternative activity for the parents; it was an alternative description of the same activity. This alternative description enabled the parents to rethink their goals for themselves.

There is no truth in the truths we have held as real

Because no reality is absolutely 'true' (see the human communication model), all meaning has been self initialised and therefore can be 'un-initialised'.

In NLP, there are two basic forms of reframes - content (or meaning) and context reframes.

The content reframe: The content of a situation can be changed to alter the meaning given to the original. An electrical power failure can be viewed as disruptive or a major disaster, given all you have to get done. Or it can be viewed as an opportunity to spend some intimate time with your spouse or to have fun with your children finding innovative ways to manage the situation. The example from Virginia Satir is an excellent example of a content reframe. All the information stays in the same place, just the meaning of that information changes.

The content reframe is useful for statements such as: "I get annoyed when my boss stands behind me while I am working". Notice how the person has taken the situation and given it a specific meaning (an arbitrary meaning) and in so doing limits her resourcefulness and possible courses of action. To reframe this situation, remember the NLP presupposition every behaviour has a positive intention and ask questions (to yourself) such as: "What other meaning could the boss's behaviour have?" Or "for what purpose does he do it?" "What is the positive value in this behaviour?" The positive value could be related to the boss's behaviour (as above) or it could be related to the speaker's behaviour.

How to powerfully deliver a reframe

Delivery of a reframe is crucial. If you were to just sit there having a chat, giving advice, it may not be as powerful as what I'm going to show you. After you have listened to the problem and got it down to a very understandable and short phrase, you ask them to listen: "Can I ask you a question that may make a difference here?" After they agree, you already have a powerful dynamic set up. Then you deliver your reframe and immediately shut up! What you are looking for here is a physiological shift in the client. And don't say a word until you have experienced what that reframe has done inside the other person.

Deliver your content reframe

Restate the problem to your client. "So you said that you get annoyed when your boss stands behind you while you are working". A possible reframe might be "Is this a chance to show off how good you are?" Or "Isn't it great that you know your boundaries and are not prepared to allow someone to violate them?" Or "good boss's like to know their staff". Of course, you'd have to get to know the person well enough before firing any random language pattern off.

And you'd get to know the situation very well beforehand also. We are not talking about positive thinking here! These reframes repatriate on an unconscious level and affect the very boundaries of the client's internal frame of reference.

If you are experiencing a physical problem (including phobias and allergies), you may ask yourself, "Is this problem useful to them in some way?" For example, it may give them permission to say "no!" If this is the case, you could ask yourself, "Is there some other way that they can get this same result without having to have the physical problem?"

Deliver your reframe

"Without this physical problem, you would never have learned the love you now have of life….when you are well, you'll have health as well as love." Or "Having this physical pattern on the outside is the healthiest way to really clear the whole thing out now". And just maybe the physical problem will disappear. It is also about finding meaning in life and finding the lessons in experiences.

An elderly woman complains of the mess her grandchildren make when they come around to see her.

Deliver your reframe

"The mess means they love being with you." If the unconscious mind likes the alternative statement, it will literally change the way it is held in the deeper mind and therefore the chemicals that go with it!

Case study

We had a delegate called Rory come to our training course one year. He had pain in his knees so much he needed a stick to aid himself walking. We found out that he had been given a 'life-sentence' early on that "when you get older, your knees go". Towards the end of the course, we had someone working with him who delivered a few reframes alongside some other good language patterns. His knee pain simply disappeared so much so that he did an Elvis impression in front of the whole room!

Let's have a review of the difference between content and context reframes.

Context reframes

Context framing is giving another meaning to a statement by changing the context you first found it in. You literally take the problem to another place where it doesn't mean the same thing anymore. A context reframe leaves the meaning of the behaviour the same and shows how the meaning will appear different when placed somewhere else.

Content reframes

If it were a picture in a frame, all the content would stay there and you'd shift the meaning of the picture's content.

A reframe is useful for statements such as: "I am too pushy." Or "I wish I did not focus on what could go wrong." In this type of situation, your client has assumed that this type of behaviour has no value. You job is to discover when it is of value by asking yourself the question: "When or where would this behaviour be useful or viewed as a resource?" A possible problem to reframe might be:

A: "I am too pushy."
B: Content reframe: "How can you use that on yourself to get more done in the day and not worry about anyone else!"

B: Context reframe: "Compared to who, Hitler?"
A: "I procrastinate all the time; I just can't get things done."
B: Content/context reframe: "That's a great skill to have; especially when you apply it to overeating - just put off having that second helping at lunch until teatime. Lucky you."
B: Context reframe: "I guess if you were building a universe, a day is a very long time!"

A: "I wish I did not focus on what could go wrong."
B: Content reframe: "Focusing your wish to the intention of the opposite is definitely a good start. I'm glad you came to see me."
B: Context reframe: "With that kind of focus you could build the best spaceship today...they need people who can spot mistakes easily!"

If you noticed, a couple of those reframes didn't really make complete grammatical sense. They are sometimes the best ones! The way to design excellent reframes is to consider all the information (knowing the person as well as you can), getting them to the smallest sentence as truthfully as it sits in their linguistic being; then letting your unconscious mind come out with the reframe and surprising you.

Chapter 17
Parts

NLP is well known for fast results and very deep personal growth - self development; but how does that happen, what's the underlying processes that allow those changes to occur?

We are going to look at this dynamic concept of synchronicity, but not just the mythical, fantasy type, we are going to look at how physics also teaches us how the world works together.

With the help of Clair Marshall who wrote most of this next piece, lets see how interconnectedness affects all of us. I have many personal examples, one of which follows:

I wanted to be in to receive a package from UPS because I had missed it the day before and would not have been able to get it if I didn't get it soon. You never know when they will arrive, so if I went out, I put up a sign with my telephone number on it so the courier could call me and I'd come right away. Just one time I slipped out for a haircut and completely forgot the note and the UPS guy.

I went into town, did a small chore at the bank and went for the haircut. The usual place was a bit busy, so I decided to go to another place. For some reason I went a route I had never taken before and after about one mile, I saw a UPS van pull out in front of me.

My alarm bells rang and I remembered my important package. But what could I do, ram the vehicle and see if it's my van with my package? The answer came quickly. The van stopped after about 50 yards and I stopped with it. I talked to the driver and hey presto, it was my van. He had been around to my house and he still had my package!

Now if you are a statistician, you can work out all the other times that DIDN'T happen and come out even over time. But have you ever PLANNED for synchronicity to occur and then witnessed it happening?

Let's look a bit deeper, (thank you to Dr. Claire Marshall for the next few paragraphs).

Interconnectedness and its Implications for the Therapeutic Relationship

Mystics, philosophers and spiritualists have long postulated that objects and people do not exist independently, and are in face connected. Recent scientific developments in quantum physics and other areas now also suggest this to be true. Psychotherapy was based on the traditional science, and with these new advances, a call for a shift in paradigm is necessary.

Defining Interconnectedness

Interconnectivity is a term used in physics, mathematics, biology and cybernetics to describe the relationship between components within a system (Wiener, 1948). This is to say that they are dependent, as well as being in communication, simply because they are integrated within the same whole. The components cannot be studied independently. To be fully understood they must be viewed in the context of their system. One example of this is an ecosystem: a self-sustaining system, where to understand part of it, for example an insect, it is necessary to know about its habitat, diet, and predators. Interconnectedness stipulates that there is a relationship between things.

The Implications of Interconnectedness

Whether or not things are connected has great implications for our view of reality. By moving from the traditional scientific perspective of separateness and isolation, to a new acknowledgment of the relationship between parts, a broader and better-informed standpoint can be assumed. One in which context is not detached from its content, and the emphasis is on relationship and interaction.

Interconnectedness in Philosophy

Contemporary philosophers Deleuze and Guattari (2004) also compare interconnectedness with the rhizome: a stem of a plant that grows horizontally. The rhizome is organized by principles of connections, with multiple points of entry and exit forming complex webs. They use the rhizome as a metaphor for the structure of things, and contrast it with a root, (which has limited structural form, is hierarchical and subsumes under a unified structure).

They compare Freud and psychoanalysis to a root complex, arguing it is fixed and mimetic. However, it is arguable that the spontaneous nature of free association does not fit with this root metaphor.

Jacques Lacan (1968), a neo-Freudian, proposed the young infant is in a state of unity with the world as it lacks the concept of a separate identity. Lacan argued language compartmentalizes life, giving it a sense of lacking, of being broken down. Piaget (1977) argued that a child develops a sense of self between two and seven years old, which is also around the time a child acquires language. This suggests that we are born with an innate, untouched knowledge of unity, however as we develop a sense of self and acquire language, this knowledge dissipates.

What has all this got to do with the NLP & Parts Integration?

The above article is relevant because we either live in a world of separateness or interconnectedness. We mostly are born into a world of negative separateness, where we are separate from our earth, our gods, and even our families to certain degrees.

To give light to this, when you have a disease process happening inside your body, do you consider that it is a part of you or completely alien and separate? Of course, for the most part we consider it to be an alien force and must be destroyed.

Yet look at the linguistics of the word itself: Dis-ease. Originally, the ancients saw a problem in the physical body as a problem of the person's self. So the person was treated for their life conditions. It was seen as the person was not at ease, hence the word dis-ease.

From those times, when disease was an integrated process, we have systematically de-tuned our view on life to a place where we are fairly happy to send high explosive weapons to wipe out another persons life if we feel they do not concur with our own.

And that is the macrocosm to the microcosm of using antibiotics to wipe our areas of the body that we feel do not belong to us!

Planet earth is a massive pool of resources that can supply everything anybody wants alongside all the health and healing properties available in plants and minerals. Yet various sections of this planet think they own these resources and can use them just for their own devices and cannot be shared around or used to develop this planet further.

Again, with the analogy of microcosm, parts can appear inside a person that has the same behaviour!

If you think of an orchestra, each part relates to the whole: if one of those parts decides not to play ball with the whole you would have a problem if you were the conductor or the audience!

Part can be formed by shock, trauma or incongruence (lack of integrity). Multiple personalities, for instance, can be formed from several parts isolating themselves to such an extent that they each have their own realities inside themselves. Indeed there have been cases where diabetes has been found in one of these multiple personalities yet not when they switch to another!

Parts Integration in NLP has an underlying presupposition that things are connected and interconnected. In other words we strive to see the purpose and higher intention of all things and how they could work together.

When a client came to see me when her hair was falling out, I asked myself "what's the connection between her life and her hair?" Also, "what's the highest intention of this behaviour of her body?" I soon found out that her life conditions were making her feel so disconnected that her beautiful hair was responding by mirroring the issue at hand. With the example used earlier of Rory and his knees, we found the life sentence that was dictating his physical condition and removed it.

When we use parts integration in NLP, we get inside the part to begin with, associated. We start to talk to the part, to notice its behaviour and nuances. Then we begin the process of chunking up (see hierarchy of ideas section), to distinguish the behaviour from the intention. We are assuming that any low level behaviour has a positive intention, so therefore the client will naturally traverse to a more complex and abstract level if questioned skilfully.

At the abstract level, all things tend to agree or are interconnected: Therefore if the mind and body come to a high level of thinking and being, they notice the role they play for the whole system. The triangle player in the orchestra suddenly remembers his or her part in the whole piece and stops sulking in the wings!

How do we separate intention from behaviour?

Use the chunking up questions from the hierarchy of ideas section to entice the person to reach higher in their experience of an event. I had an issue with my hobby of fishing. On the one hand I love being in nature, with water and all the wonderful things that you see early in the morning and late at night. Fishing allowed me to be close to the earth for a whole day or even longer, whilst having a focus I enjoy.

On the other hand, it's a very strange thing to do. Pulling fish out of their habitat whilst seducing them with food, them putting them back after the experience is a little odd!

To release the oddness of pulling fish out (the behaviour), I started to chunk up on each part. For the problem part I asked myself who it may be? It was represented by my father (for whatever reason I don't know as he had no issue with fishing). I asked the part "for what intention do you disagree?" It answered, "to show you that it's strange". I asked again, "what's the purpose of pointing out that it's strange?" Another answer; "to keep you doing what's right." Question: "What's the purpose of doing what's right?" Answer: "To keep you aligned with everything in life." Question "What will that get for me?" Answer: "The knowledge of always knowing you are at one with things."

I chunked up the other part (that has no problem with fishing, the opposite of the other). It came to the same place quite quickly.

When parts then begin to experience that they are not at all disconnected and are part of the whole, they soon loosen their position and can integrate.

Chapter 18
Time Based Techniques

The evolution of Time-Based Techniques has come about naturally as a result of using NLP in a more flexible way. Therefore, we have come to a time where these processes work even quicker than ever before:

The approximate time required to release a significant emotional experience (SEE) for a client with different forms of therapy are as follows: -

Freudian - 100 hours to five years!
Behavioural - 10 weeks
Ericksonian - 15 hour
Time Line Therapy - 4 hours or more
Time-Based Techniques - 2 hours or less

So what's special about Time Based Techniques (TBT) and how does one work with time?

The Concept of Time

Humans unconsciously store memories and know the difference between a memory from the past and a projection of the future.

That has to be true otherwise you wouldn't know the difference between tomorrow, today or yesterday!

Yet, saying that, all that really is occurring happens in the now. The past has gone, the future is not here yet. NOW is what we are working with. Even if their is a past issue, that issue is happening NOW.

Therefore all time based challenges are built of CONCEPTS of time. Knowing that will/can revolutionise the way you work with people (and, of course yourself).

If you can get your clients into the NOW whilst still experiencing the issues, you will be 80% of the way towards completing the issues. Most past problems are problems because the memories got stuck and then got isolated. All the wisdom, experience and learning since the problem has not been integrated.

The work you are doing with your client is to open up that memory and expose it to the NOW, with all the experience NOW had to offer. If you think about it, the issues would not be issues if the unconscious mind didn't know any better! If the unconscious/higher mind knows better it ALREADY knows solutions! You've just got to get the other person to be PRESENT enough to experience all of this.

That's where Time Based Techniques becomes so very useful.

Behavioural change in an individual takes place at an unconscious level. People don't change consciously. Therefore you have to project your questions and intention towards the unconscious mind for maximum effect. Then you can see quicker results. Time Based Techniques allow you to work at the unconscious level and release the effects of past negative experiences and change 'inappropriate' programming in minutes rather than days, months or years.

Some other Time Techniques are mostly based on visual models to work with. With TBT that has changed that so now practitioners can work with time travel in any of the senses (VAKOG Ai).

Also the 'travelling' part is made super easy by a simple-to-use technique where a practitioner harnesses the modalities mentioned above to instantaneously transport clients to anywhere in this lifetime or past lifetimes, if that's where the problems arose.

TBT has done away with the concept that there is just one 'root cause' as well. You can use any of the memories that the client's unconscious comes up with, from the presenting problem to past lives.

The whole process works in a similar way to conversational

anchoring, to be utilized in a conversation...and not stop the client to set up a difficult process. We tend to use the client's own inner emotions and clues to let us know what modality (Visual, Audio, etc), to travel back in...and it will happen in the moment.

In NLP we say that naturally occurring states are the most powerful, so why stop the client if they are already accessing a powerful state? *"ummm, excuse me, I see that you are going into an emotion...let's set up the technique I am going to use"* ??!! Then, in the old methods, you'd spend 30 minutes telling them how the process will work.

With Time Based Techniques, the practitioner doesn't stop the flow at all but simply uses the client's physiology and other 'spots' to let them know what modality to travel back with and do it in the moment, utilizing a naturally occurring state!

I give credit here to John Overdurf and Julie Silverthorne, who evolved TBT.

Time Based Techniques are based on guiding the client to their own learnings that are always there to replace the problem. This leads the client to be empowered to use the techniques successfully, have the experience of doing it themselves and have the permanent experience of the emotion or limiting belief being banished forever.

How do you work with a client and time?

A) Letting a feeling, sound or self talk guide them back.
B) Walking the Time Line.

A) Using conversational Time Based Techniques

Find the Event: Watch your client for clues to which way will work the best to travel back in time: Some pointers will be the eyes patterns, flushing of the face, physiology of the body, voice changes. Use the modality they are in to travel back with.

Always ask: "Is it all right for your Unconscious Mind for you to release this (emotion or limiting decision) today and for you to be aware of it consciously?"

Then have a 'chat' (they will think it's just a chat), about the issue. Watch your client for clues to which way will work the best to travel back in time: (i.e. VAKOG & Ai).

For instance, when you see your client experiencing an emotion, check out if they are experiencing that in visual way or through their thoughts, audio etc. Watch the eye patterns and calibrate. If they are in thoughts, ask them to use that thought to take them back to the earliest possible memory (it can be any memory - trust their unconscious mind), and wait until they come to a conscious reliving of that memory. See the scripts on page 194 for more wording.

Walking the Time Line

This is good for people who don't have good abstract minds or who have to do things physically. Get them to imagine a line across a room. You can 'walk' it out for them to get a feel for it first. Have a present moment place in the middle and a past and future (make sure there's plenty of room for he past to go back). Tell them that this is the entirety of their life span (or lives).

Then get them to walk back along the line, until their unconscious mind (or deeper mind) gives them a sign that something is significant at some point. The deeper mind can give them an internal feeling or even wobble them on the journey.

At that point, ask them "what's happening?" They may not know consciously, so direct the question to their unconscious mind. Then, when the client starts to talk about the event, you can use your other NLP skills to reframe/retranslate the problem event.

Scripts and processes

When you see your client accessing the problem state, you can start the time travelling process:

"Let this feeling (sound, picture, thought, feeling) take you back to the earliest time, which when accessed will allow the problem to disappear. Let me know when you are there by nodding your head" "OK, *now* you are there, what have you learned *now*, that will allow this old problem to disappear?"

"Through all your experiences since this event, allow the understandings and experiences to reframe that old problem, until the emotion completely disappears from it. *Will it to happen* that it just reframes, in the light of this new view?"

"What can you notice differently about that old problem *now*, and what angles can you view it from now, so that it has changed itself.....and you can keep the change!"

(At his point you can use perceptual positions to reframe the old memory. Get them to go inside other people, float above the event...anything which changes the perspective.)

NOTES:
•   If client says "I don't know what or where the event is"

after you can clearly see they are in it, then respond with "I know you don't, but if you did...take whatever comes up...trust your unconscious mind."

• Ratify the change: Verify conscious acknowledgment of shift. When a major physiological shift occurs in the client, be sure to mention it: "That was a big one, wasn't it?"

One of the things I love about TBT is that it incorporates almost all of your NLP skills. That's why I have listed it lastly here in the book as a technique.

John Overdurf & Julie Silverthorne (who evolved TBT) would not always class TBT as a stand alone technique, just as much as we wouldn't have a separate heading or trademark for Submodalities. It's just be way of integrating all the facilities inside your NLP toolbox. And that's a good place to end this book, on the premise that TBT and NLP (along with all the other change techniques I use), do not work alone or isolated.

There are many reasons that your client has come to see you. Sometimes it may be a spiritual re-evaluation of their life. What they tell you is that their dog died and they can't get over it; yet you will just be looking for clues to what's really happening here inside.

When you eventually find the 'real' problem, you have many, many options. You may also feel, in the moment, to mix and match some techniques together to create a change for the client.

When you are comfortable enough to see NLP or any techniques as partly what will work, you are on your way to being an excellent practitioner. Then you will work quickly and efficiently.

So, when it comes to change, what's really happening? You may now come to the understanding that the setup, your sensory awareness, your ability to create rapport and your flexibility of approach are the cornerstones of any good work you'll ever do.

With that in your pocket, the techniques of NLP become secondary to HOW you are thinking about the whole process of change. I trust this has been valuable to you to promote and empower the changes for your clients and yourself...and you can keep the change!

GLOSSARY

This glossary is by no means exhaustive, but it does give a few short definitions of some NLP terms and should make the language of NLP a little easier to internalise. For a much more comprehensive glossary look at www.nlpworld.co.uk

Accessing Cues
Slight changes in breathing, posture, gestures and eye movements that show internal mental processing such as visualisation, auditory and kinaesthetic activity. Watching out for these helps the observer assess the congruence of the actor with ideas presented to him.

Anchoring
The process of associating an internal response with an external trigger so that by applying a gesture, touch, sound or smell just before a state peaks, either in oneself or someone else, the anchored state can be re-activated by reapplying that gesture, touch, sound or smell.

Associated
Looking through your own eyes, hearing what you heard, feeling what you felt, smelling what you smelled as intensely as if you were actually there is associating.
Away from

One of the filters which describe how we make choices about situations. Some people are very 'away from' in that they like to move away from a situation rather than moving towards a more positive one. Knowing how children react in this way makes constructing behaviour programmes more effective because you can use carrots and sticks according to whether they respond to towards stimuli or away from.

Calibration
The skill of recognising visible, auditory and kinaesthetic 'facts' from a person, rather than mind reading their body language.

Congruence
When all of a person's internal beliefs, strategies, and behaviours are fully in agreement with their verbal output whilst communicating. Convincing people will appear normal and natural when their body language sits comfortably with what they are saying.

Content reframing
Changing your response to an experience by changing the meaning you give to it.

Context reframing
Taking an event to another place so that the meaning changes by that movement.

Embedded commands
Instructions that are subtly included in speech, but marked out by changing the voice tone (deeper and louder).

Deletion
A way of coping with the mass of information the brain is presented with every second. For instance, we all have deleted the mass of

pixels that are all around us, all the time. The small stain on the desk is not noticed in the chaos of the class (if you are noticing it, then you are probably too relaxed)!

Dissociation
Looking at your body from an outside position and experiencing the world from outside your own physical position so that you do not have the feelings you would have if you were actually there. Being able to be dispassionate about an emotional situation.

Distortion
A way the human brain copes with large amounts of information constantly bombarding it. Events are represented differently from the real world making them fit in more easily with existing patterns. Teachers are experts at being able to distort the briefs given to them (which are sometimes impossible), to be able to make the results really happen!

Ecology
Ecology is the consideration of effects of changes that could happen if a goal is achieved. The ecology of a goal for instance would include family, partners, colleagues, as well as possible effects on the physical environment.

Future Pace
The process of mentally rehearsing a situation in the future, to ensure a positive outcome.

Generalisation
A way the brain copes with the mass of information it is presented with by taking a specific incident or behaviour and generalising it across contexts.

Incongruence
A divided response indicating reservation and a not total commitment to an outcome. The words do not match the actions. The body does not reflect the speaking.

Intention
The purpose or outcome of any behaviour.

Internal representation
The pictures, sounds and feelings that we make on the inside; our thoughts. The way we store and sort our memories in a kind of mental map.

Leading
The process of gaining sufficient rapport with another to lead their behaviour using both verbal and non-verbal communication to elicit a desired response from another person.

Lead system
The preferred representational system -visual, auditory, kinaesthetic- that takes information from the exterior. Usually outside conscious awareness. Can detect via someone's eye patterns.

Matching
Adopting parts of another person's behaviour and language preferences to enhance rapport.

Meta Model
The Meta Model provides questions to elicit lost information which previously was distorted, generalised and deleted.

Metaphor
Stories, parables, analogies, allegories that enable the unconscious

mind to understand new things. These methods tap directly into the unconscious mind enabling learning through the unconscious mind.

Milton Model
The 'artfully vague' language to induce confusion or uncertainty in another's listening. Used to by-pass the conscious guards of disbelief. Based on the language used by hypnotherapist Milton H. Erickson M.D. It is the complement to the precise Meta Model, deliberately generalizing, distorting and deleting content.

Modelling
The process of observing, replicating and mapping the successful behaviours of other people.

Outcomes
Goals or desired states that a person or organization aspires to achieve, framed in positive terms and within the individuals ambit.

Nominalisation
A verb which has been turned into an abstract noun. e.g. 'learnings' is a nomilisation because we have not defined the word before using it.

Pacing
A method used by excellent communicators to quickly establish rapport by matching certain aspects of their behaviour to those of the person with whom they are communicating - a matching or mirroring of behaviour.

Preferred/Primary Representation System
The representational system that an individual uses to express their internal world.

Presupposition

A basic underlying assumption that is necessary for an internal representation to make sense e.g. "Well you have done this before so you can easily do it again", presupposes you can. "If you sit in this learning chair, learning becomes twice as fast". As long as there is enough rapport for someone to consider a truth in what you are saying, then the presuppositions will work! Often a presupposition is outside a person's conscious awareness.

Perceptions

The half full/half empty glass. We can interpret this as:

If you want more, it is half empty; if you have had enough, it is half full. We cannot change how much is in the glass, only the way we think about it.

Rapport

The establishment of trust, harmony, and cooperation in a relationship. Groups can be in rapport and show this by synchronized behaviour. Rapport can be gained by matching body language and behaviour.

Reframing (see also content and context reframes)

Changing the meaning of a situation by putting a different frame or perspective on one's thoughts about it e.g. "I have no money". Challenge, "compared to who, the guy in the shop doorway?"

Resource

Anything that adds to the achievement of an outcome, so it could be a belief, understanding, piece of knowledge. Any internal or external assistance. In NLP we tend to guide others to knowing they have access to all resources.

Sensory acuity/awareness
The process of learning to make finer and more useful distinctions about the information we get from the world by attending to fine changes in physiology of another. Information that can be used to calibrate (make factual observations) on another.

Unconscious mind (sub-dominant or 'not' the conscious mind)
Mental processes outside conscious awareness. The majority of one's learning takes place in the unconscious mind, so as teachers, it's a good idea to see how well you are relating to this area in your teaching skills. Also the conscious mind can only handle very small amounts of information, so you'll need to provide small packages to allow learning to occur. Either that, or learn how to use NLP more proficiently to access deeper areas of learning; more colourful, more sensory based, to appeal to the sub-dominant or unconscious mind. For example, you can put across untold amounts of information in a metaphor as opposed to about 5 key points in plain, logical fact.

.

YOUR FREE GIFTS FROM TERRY ELSTON & NLP WORLD

Free coaching with audio and video tips from NLP World
http://www.nlpworld.co.uk/nlp-online-bronze-trial-package

The book Think and Grow Rich has been a best seller, with over 7 million copies sold worldwide.

To compliment the learning's you may have established here, NLP World has made a copy available to you.

You will find a free download at:
www.nlpworld.co.uk/media/zips/Think-And-Grow-Rich_NLPWorld-Edition.zip

Please contact me if you have any other questions
terryelston@nlpworld.co.uk
www.nlpworld.co.uk